THE OFFICIAL PATIENT'S SOURCEBOOK

on

APRAXIA

JAMES N. PARKER, M.D.
AND PHILIP M. PARKER, PH.D., EDITORS

ICON Health Publications
ICON Group International, Inc.
4370 La Jolla Village Drive, 4th Floor
San Diego, CA 92122 USA

Printed in the United States of America.

Last digit indicates print number: 10 9 8 7 6 4 5 3 2 1

Publisher, Health Care: Tiffany LaRochelle
Editor(s): James Parker, M.D., Philip Parker, Ph.D.

Publisher's note: The ideas, procedures, and suggestions contained in this book are not intended as a substitute for consultation with your physician. All matters regarding your health require medical supervision. As new medical or scientific information becomes available from academic and clinical research, recommended treatments and drug therapies may undergo changes. The authors, editors, and publisher have attempted to make the information in this book up to date and accurate in accord with accepted standards at the time of publication. The authors, editors, and publisher are not responsible for errors or omissions or for consequences from application of the book, and make no warranty, expressed or implied, in regard to the contents of this book. Any practice described in this book should be applied by the reader in accordance with professional standards of care used in regard to the unique circumstances that may apply in each situation, in close consultation with a qualified physician. The reader is advised to always check product information (package inserts) for changes and new information regarding dose and contraindications before taking any drug or pharmacological product. Caution is especially urged when using new or infrequently ordered drugs, herbal remedies, vitamins and supplements, alternative therapies, complementary therapies and medicines, and integrative medical treatments.

Cataloging-in-Publication Data

Parker, James N., 1961-
Parker, Philip M., 1960-

The Official Patient's Sourcebook on Apraxia: A Revised and Updated Directory for the Internet Age/James N. Parker and Philip M. Parker, editors
        p.   cm.
Includes bibliographical references, glossary and index.
ISBN: 0-597-83046-0
1. Apraxia-Popular works.   I. Title.

Disclaimer

This publication is not intended to be used for the diagnosis or treatment of a health problem or as a substitute for consultation with licensed medical professionals. It is sold with the understanding that the publisher, editors, and authors are not engaging in the rendering of medical, psychological, financial, legal, or other professional services.

References to any entity, product, service, or source of information that may be contained in this publication should not be considered an endorsement, either direct or implied, by the publisher, editors or authors. ICON Group International, Inc., the editors, or the authors are not responsible for the content of any Web pages nor publications referenced in this publication.

Copyright Notice

Dedication

To the healthcare professionals dedicating their time and efforts to the study of apraxia.

Acknowledgements

The collective knowledge generated from academic and applied research summarized in various references has been critical in the creation of this sourcebook which is best viewed as a comprehensive compilation and collection of information prepared by various official agencies which directly or indirectly are dedicated to apraxia. All of the *Official Patient's Sourcebooks* draw from various agencies and institutions associated with the United States Department of Health and Human Services, and in particular, the Office of the Secretary of Health and Human Services (OS), the Administration for Children and Families (ACF), the Administration on Aging (AOA), the Agency for Healthcare Research and Quality (AHRQ), the Agency for Toxic Substances and Disease Registry (ATSDR), the Centers for Disease Control and Prevention (CDC), the Food and Drug Administration (FDA), the Healthcare Financing Administration (HCFA), the Health Resources and Services Administration (HRSA), the Indian Health Service (IHS), the institutions of the National Institutes of Health (NIH), the Program Support Center (PSC), and the Substance Abuse and Mental Health Services Administration (SAMHSA). In addition to these sources, information gathered from the National Library of Medicine, the United States Patent Office, the European Union, and their related organizations has been invaluable in the creation of this sourcebook. Some of the work represented was financially supported by the Research and Development Committee at INSEAD. This support is gratefully acknowledged. Finally, special thanks are owed to Tiffany LaRochelle for her excellent editorial support.

About the Editors

James N. Parker, M.D.

Dr. James N. Parker received his Bachelor of Science degree in Psychobiology from the University of California, Riverside and his M.D. from the University of California, San Diego. In addition to authoring numerous research publications, he has lectured at various academic institutions. Dr. Parker is the medical editor for the *Official Patient's Sourcebook* series published by ICON Health Publications.

Philip M. Parker, Ph.D.

Philip M. Parker is the Eli Lilly Chair Professor of Innovation, Business and Society at INSEAD (Fontainebleau, France and Singapore). Dr. Parker has also been Professor at the University of California, San Diego and has taught courses at Harvard University, the Hong Kong University of Science and Technology, the Massachusetts Institute of Technology, Stanford University, and UCLA. Dr. Parker is the associate editor for the *Official Patient's Sourcebook* series published by ICON Health Publications.

About ICON Health Publications

In addition to apraxia, *Official Patient's Sourcebooks* are available for the following related topics:

- The Official Patient's Sourcebook on Benign Essential Blepharospasm
- The Official Patient's Sourcebook on Dermatomyositis
- The Official Patient's Sourcebook on Dystonia Disorders
- The Official Patient's Sourcebook on Fahr's Syndrome
- The Official Patient's Sourcebook on Guillain-barre
- The Official Patient's Sourcebook on Hemifacial Spasm
- The Official Patient's Sourcebook on Huntington's Disease
- The Official Patient's Sourcebook on Inclusion Body Myositis
- The Official Patient's Sourcebook on Miller Fisher Syndrome
- The Official Patient's Sourcebook on Multifocal Motor Neuropathy
- The Official Patient's Sourcebook on Multiple Sclerosis
- The Official Patient's Sourcebook on Myasthenia Gravis
- The Official Patient's Sourcebook on Myoclonus
- The Official Patient's Sourcebook on Opsoclonus Myoclonus
- The Official Patient's Sourcebook on Parkinson's Disease
- The Official Patient's Sourcebook on Parry Romberg
- The Official Patient's Sourcebook on Periodic Paralyses
- The Official Patient's Sourcebook on Polymyositis
- The Official Patient's Sourcebook on Progressive Supranuclear Palsy
- The Official Patient's Sourcebook on Ramsey Hunt Syndrome Type II
- The Official Patient's Sourcebook on Spasticity
- The Official Patient's Sourcebook on Stiff Person Syndrome
- The Official Patient's Sourcebook on Tardive Dyskinesia
- The Official Patient's Sourcebook on Tremor

To discover more about ICON Health Publications, simply check with your preferred online booksellers, including Barnes & Noble.com and Amazon.com which currently carry all of our titles. Or, feel free to contact us directly for bulk purchases or institutional discounts:

ICON Group International, Inc.
4370 La Jolla Village Drive, Fourth Floor
San Diego, CA 92122 USA
Fax: 858-546-4341
Web site: **www.icongrouponline.com/health**

Table of Contents

INTRODUCTION

Overview

Dr. C. Everett Koop, former U.S. Surgeon General, once said, "The best prescription is knowledge."[1] The Agency for Healthcare Research and Quality (AHRQ) of the National Institutes of Health (NIH) echoes this view and recommends that every patient incorporate education into the treatment process. According to the AHRQ:

> Finding out more about your condition is a good place to start. By contacting groups that support your condition, visiting your local library, and searching on the Internet, you can find good information to help guide your treatment decisions. Some information may be hard to find — especially if you don't know where to look.[2]

As the AHRQ mentions, finding the right information is not an obvious task. Though many physicians and public officials had thought that the emergence of the Internet would do much to assist patients in obtaining reliable information, in March 2001 the National Institutes of Health issued the following warning:

> The number of Web sites offering health-related resources grows every day. Many sites provide valuable information, while others may have information that is unreliable or misleading.[3]

---

[1] Quotation from **http://www.drkoop.com**.

[2] The Agency for Healthcare Research and Quality (AHRQ):
http://www.ahcpr.gov/consumer/diaginfo.htm.

[3] From the NIH, National Cancer Institute (NCI):
http://cancertrials.nci.nih.gov/beyond/evaluating.html.

Since the late 1990s, physicians have seen a general increase in patient Internet usage rates. Patients frequently enter their doctor's offices with printed Web pages of home remedies in the guise of latest medical research. This scenario is so common that doctors often spend more time dispelling misleading information than guiding patients through sound therapies. *The Official Patient's Sourcebook on Apraxia* has been created for patients who have decided to make education and research an integral part of the treatment process. The pages that follow will tell you where and how to look for information covering virtually all topics related to apraxia, from the essentials to the most advanced areas of research.

The title of this book includes the word "official." This reflects the fact that the sourcebook draws from public, academic, government, and peer-reviewed research. Selected readings from various agencies are reproduced to give you some of the latest official information available to date on apraxia.

Given patients' increasing sophistication in using the Internet, abundant references to reliable Internet-based resources are provided throughout this sourcebook. Where possible, guidance is provided on how to obtain free-of-charge, primary research results as well as more detailed information via the Internet. E-book and electronic versions of this sourcebook are fully interactive with each of the Internet sites mentioned (clicking on a hyperlink automatically opens your browser to the site indicated). Hard copy users of this sourcebook can type cited Web addresses directly into their browsers to obtain access to the corresponding sites. Since we are working with ICON Health Publications, hard copy *Sourcebooks* are frequently updated and printed on demand to ensure that the information provided is current.

In addition to extensive references accessible via the Internet, every chapter presents a "Vocabulary Builder." Many health guides offer glossaries of technical or uncommon terms in an appendix. In editing this sourcebook, we have decided to place a smaller glossary within each chapter that covers terms used in that chapter. Given the technical nature of some chapters, you may need to revisit many sections. Building one's vocabulary of medical terms in such a gradual manner has been shown to improve the learning process.

We must emphasize that no sourcebook on apraxia should affirm that a specific diagnostic procedure or treatment discussed in a research study, patent, or doctoral dissertation is "correct" or your best option. This sourcebook is no exception. Each patient is unique. Deciding on appropriate options is always up to the patient in consultation with their physician and healthcare providers.

Organization

This sourcebook is organized into three parts. Part I explores basic techniques to researching apraxia (e.g. finding guidelines on diagnosis, treatments, and prognosis), followed by a number of topics, including information on how to get in touch with organizations, associations, or other patient networks dedicated to apraxia. It also gives you sources of information that can help you find a doctor in your local area specializing in treating apraxia. Collectively, the material presented in Part I is a complete primer on basic research topics for patients with apraxia.

Part II moves on to advanced research dedicated to apraxia. Part II is intended for those willing to invest many hours of hard work and study. It is here that we direct you to the latest scientific and applied research on apraxia. When possible, contact names, links via the Internet, and summaries are provided. It is in Part II where the vocabulary process becomes important as authors publishing advanced research frequently use highly specialized language. In general, every attempt is made to recommend "free-to-use" options.

Part III provides appendices of useful background reading for all patients with apraxia or related disorders. The appendices are dedicated to more pragmatic issues faced by many patients with apraxia. Accessing materials via medical libraries may be the only option for some readers, so a guide is provided for finding local medical libraries which are open to the public. Part III, therefore, focuses on advice that goes beyond the biological and scientific issues facing patients with apraxia.

Scope

While this sourcebook covers apraxia, your doctor, research publications, and specialists may refer to your condition using a variety of terms. Therefore, you should understand that apraxia is often considered a synonym or a condition closely related to the following:

- Cogan's Syndrome, Type Ii
- Congenital Oculomotor Apraxia

In addition to synonyms and related conditions, physicians may refer to apraxia using certain coding systems. The International Classification of Diseases, 9th Revision, Clinical Modification (ICD-9-CM) is the most commonly used system of classification for the world's illnesses. Your physician may use this coding system as an administrative or tracking tool. The following classification is commonly used for apraxia:[4]

- 438.81 apraxia
- 784.69 apraxia

For the purposes of this sourcebook, we have attempted to be as inclusive as possible, looking for official information for all of the synonyms relevant to apraxia. You may find it useful to refer to synonyms when accessing databases or interacting with healthcare professionals and medical librarians.

Moving Forward

Since the 1980s, the world has seen a proliferation of healthcare guides covering most illnesses. Some are written by patients or their family members. These generally take a layperson's approach to understanding and coping with an illness or disorder. They can be uplifting, encouraging, and highly supportive. Other guides are authored by physicians or other healthcare providers who have a more clinical outlook. Each of these two styles of guide has its purpose and can be quite useful.

As editors, we have chosen a third route. We have chosen to expose you to as many sources of official and peer-reviewed information as practical, for the purpose of educating you about basic and advanced knowledge as recognized by medical science today. You can think of this sourcebook as your personal Internet age reference librarian.

Why "Internet age"? All too often, patients diagnosed with apraxia will log on to the Internet, type words into a search engine, and receive several Web site listings which are mostly irrelevant or redundant. These patients are left to wonder where the relevant information is, and how to obtain it. Since only the smallest fraction of information dealing with apraxia is even indexed in

---

[4] This list is based on the official version of the World Health Organization's 9th Revision, International Classification of Diseases (ICD-9). According to the National Technical Information Service, "ICD-9CM extensions, interpretations, modifications, addenda, or errata other than those approved by the U.S. Public Health Service and the Health Care Financing Administration are not to be considered official and should not be utilized. Continuous maintenance of the ICD-9-CM is the responsibility of the federal government."

search engines, a non-systematic approach often leads to frustration and disappointment. With this sourcebook, we hope to direct you to the information you need that you would not likely find using popular Web directories. Beyond Web listings, in many cases we will reproduce brief summaries or abstracts of available reference materials. These abstracts often contain distilled information on topics of discussion.

While we focus on the more scientific aspects of apraxia, there is, of course, the emotional side to consider. Later in the sourcebook, we provide a chapter dedicated to helping you find peer groups and associations that can provide additional support beyond research produced by medical science. We hope that the choices we have made give you the most options available in moving forward. In this way, we wish you the best in your efforts to incorporate this educational approach into your treatment plan.

The Editors

PART I: THE ESSENTIALS

ABOUT PART I

Part I has been edited to give you access to what we feel are "the essentials" on apraxia. The essentials of a disease typically include the definition or description of the disease, a discussion of who it affects, the signs or symptoms associated with the disease, tests or diagnostic procedures that might be specific to the disease, and treatments for the disease. Your doctor or healthcare provider may have already explained the essentials of apraxia to you or even given you a pamphlet or brochure describing apraxia. Now you are searching for more in-depth information. As editors, we have decided, nevertheless, to include a discussion on where to find essential information that can complement what your doctor has already told you. In this section we recommend a process, not a particular Web site or reference book. The process ensures that, as you search the Web, you gain background information in such a way as to maximize your understanding.

CHAPTER 1. THE ESSENTIALS ON APRAXIA: GUIDELINES

Overview

Official agencies, as well as federally-funded institutions supported by national grants, frequently publish a variety of guidelines on apraxia. These are typically called "Fact Sheets" or "Guidelines." They can take the form of a brochure, information kit, pamphlet, or flyer. Often they are only a few pages in length. The great advantage of guidelines over other sources is that they are often written with the patient in mind. Since new guidelines on apraxia can appear at any moment and be published by a number of sources, the best approach to finding guidelines is to systematically scan the Internet-based services that post them.

The National Institutes of Health (NIH)[5]

The National Institutes of Health (NIH) is the first place to search for relatively current patient guidelines and fact sheets on apraxia. Originally founded in 1887, the NIH is one of the world's foremost medical research centers and the federal focal point for medical research in the United States. At any given time, the NIH supports some 35,000 research grants at universities, medical schools, and other research and training institutions, both nationally and internationally. The rosters of those who have conducted research or who have received NIH support over the years include the world's most illustrious scientists and physicians. Among them are 97 scientists who have won the Nobel Prize for achievement in medicine.

---

[5] Adapted from the NIH: **http://www.nih.gov/about/NIHoverview.html**.

There is no guarantee that any one Institute will have a guideline on a specific disease, though the National Institutes of Health collectively publish over 600 guidelines for both common and rare diseases. The best way to access NIH guidelines is via the Internet. Although the NIH is organized into many different Institutes and Offices, the following is a list of key Web sites where you are most likely to find NIH clinical guidelines and publications dealing with apraxia and associated conditions:

- Office of the Director (OD); guidelines consolidated across agencies available at **http://www.nih.gov/health/consumer/conkey.htm**

- National Library of Medicine (NLM); extensive encyclopedia (A.D.A.M., Inc.) with guidelines available at **http://www.nlm.nih.gov/medlineplus/healthtopics.html**

- National Institute of Neurological Disorders and Stroke (NINDS); **http://www.ninds.nih.gov/health_and_medical/disorder_index.htm**

Among the above, the National Institute of Neurological Disorders and Stroke (NINDS) is particularly noteworthy. The mission of the NINDS is to reduce the burden of neurological disease—a burden borne by every age group, by every segment of society, by people all over the world.[6] To support this mission, the NINDS conducts, fosters, coordinates, and guides research on the causes, prevention, diagnosis, and treatment of neurological disorders and stroke, and supports basic research in related scientific areas. The following patient guideline was recently published by the NINDS on apraxia.

What Is Apraxia?[7]

Apraxia is a neurological disorder characterized by loss of the ability to execute or carry out learned (familiar) movements, despite having the desire and the physical ability to perform the movements. There are several types of apraxia including limb-kinetic (inability to make fine, precise movements with a limb), ideomotor (inability to carry out a motor command), ideational (inability to create a plan for or idea of a specific movement), buccofacial or facial-oral (inability to carry out facial movements on command, i.e., lick lips, whistle, cough, or wink) which is perhaps the most common form, verbal

---

[6] This paragraph has been adapted from the NINDS: **http://www.ninds.nih.gov/about_ninds/mission.htm**. "Adapted" signifies that a passage has been reproduced exactly or slightly edited for this book.

[7] Adapted from The National Institute of Neurological Disorders and Stroke (NINDS): **http://www.ninds.nih.gov/health_and_medical/disorders/apraxia.htm**.

(difficulty coordinating mouth and speech movements), constructional (inability to draw or construct simple configurations), and oculomotor (difficulty moving the eyes). Apraxia may be accompanied by a language disorder called aphasia.

Is There Any Treatment?

Generally, treatment for individuals with apraxia includes physical and or occupational therapy. If apraxia is a symptom of another disorder, the underlying disorder should be treated.

What Is the Prognosis?

The prognosis for individuals with apraxia varies. With therapy, some patients improve significantly, while others may show very little improvement.

What Research Is Being Done?

The NINDS supports research on movement disorders such as apraxia. The goals of this research are to increase scientific understanding of these disorders, and to fine ways to prevent, treat, and cure them.

For More Information

For more information, contact:

> **Worldwide Education & Awareness for Movement Disorders (WE MOVE)**
> 204 West 84th Street
> New York, NY 10024
> wemove@wemove.org
> **http://www.wemove.org**
> Tel: 800-437-MOV2 (6682) / 212-875-8312
> Fax: 212-875-8389

More Guideline Sources

The guideline above on apraxia is only one example of the kind of material that you can find online and free of charge. The remainder of this chapter will direct you to other sources which either publish or can help you find additional guidelines on topics related to apraxia. Many of the guidelines listed below address topics that may be of particular relevance to your specific situation or of special interest to only some patients with apraxia. Due to space limitations these sources are listed in a concise manner. Do not hesitate to consult the following sources by either using the Internet hyperlink provided, or, in cases where the contact information is provided, contacting the publisher or author directly.

Topic Pages: MEDLINEplus

For patients wishing to go beyond guidelines published by specific Institutes of the NIH, the National Library of Medicine has created a vast and patient-oriented healthcare information portal called MEDLINEplus. Within this Internet-based system are "health topic pages." You can think of a health topic page as a guide to patient guides. To access this system, log on to **http://www.nlm.nih.gov/medlineplus/healthtopics.html**. From there you can either search using the alphabetical index or browse by broad topic areas.

If you do not find topics of interest when browsing health topic pages, then you can choose to use the advanced search utility of MEDLINEplus at **http://www.nlm.nih.gov/medlineplus/advancedsearch.html**. This utility is similar to the NIH Search Utility, with the exception that it only includes material linked within the MEDLINEplus system (mostly patient-oriented information). It also has the disadvantage of generating unstructured results. We recommend, therefore, that you use this method only if you have a very targeted search.

The Combined Health Information Database (CHID)

CHID Online is a reference tool that maintains a database directory of thousands of journal articles and patient education guidelines on apraxia and related conditions. One of the advantages of CHID over other sources is that it offers summaries that describe the guidelines available, including contact information and pricing. CHID's general Web site is **http://chid.nih.gov/**.   To   search   this   database,   go   to

http://chid.nih.gov/detail/detail.html. In particular, you can use the advanced search options to look up pamphlets, reports, brochures, and information kits. The following was recently posted in this archive:

- **Rett Syndrome**

  Source: Bethesda, MD: National Institute of Neurological Disorders and Stroke, National Institutes of Health. 2000. 15 p.

  Contact: Available from National Institute of Neurological Disorders and Stroke. P.O. Box 5801, Bethesda, MD 20824. (800) 352-9424. Website: www.ninds.nih.gov. Price: Single copy free.

  Summary: Rett syndrome is a childhood neurodevelopmental disorder characterized by normal early development followed by loss of purposeful use of the hands, distinctive hand movements, slowed brain and head growth, gait abnormalities, seizures, and mental retardation; it affects females almost exclusively. This brochure reviews the diagnosis and management of children with Rett syndrome. Hypotonia (loss of muscle tone) is usually the first symptom. As the syndrome progresses, the child loses purposeful use of her hands and the ability to speak. Another symptom, apraxia (the inability to perform motor functions) is perhaps the most severely disabling feature of Rett syndrome, interfering with every body movement, including eye gaze and speech. The brochure reviews the four stages of Rett syndrome, the genetic causes of Rett syndrome, epidemiology, diagnostic tests, the varied course and severity, treatment options, and prognosis. Treatment for the disorder is symptomatic, focusing on the management of symptoms, and supportive, requiring a multidisciplinary approach. Despite the difficulties with symptoms, most people with Rett syndrome continue to live well into middle age and beyond. Because the disorder is rare, little is known about long term prognosis and life expectancy. The brochure briefly summarizes the research presently being done by the Federal Government through two of the National Institutes of Health. The brochure concludes with a list of resource organizations through which readers can obtain additional information.

- **Communication for a Lifetime: Speech, Language, and Hearing in the Older Adult**

  Source: Rockville, MD: American Speech-Language-Hearing Association (ASHA). 200x. 12 p.

  Contact: Available from American Speech-Language-Hearing Association (ASHA). Product Sales, 10801 Rockville Pike, Rockville, MD 20852. (888)

498-6699. TTY (301) 897-0157. Website: www.asha.org. Price: $4.00 for 10, plus shipping and handling. Item Number: 0210105.

Summary: This brochure reviews the typical changes in communication abilities that can accompany aging. The brochure emphasizes that knowing about speech, language, and hearing disorders can prevent or reduce the impact of any losses and enhance the ability to continue a happy and healthy life. The brochure offers facts about aging and hearing loss, including the statistics of hearing loss, its typical causes, and the impact of hearing loss on everyday life. The brochure then reviews the same type of information for speech and language disorders, including aphasia (reduced understanding of language), dysarthria (a nervous system of muscle disorder that makes speech hard for others to understand), apraxia of speech (difficulty coordinating the muscles of speech), cognitive communication impairments, laryngectomy (removal of the larynx, or voice box), and dysphagia (swallowing disorder). The brochure concludes by encouraging readers who have concerns about speech language or swallowing impairments to consult a speech language pathologist for an evaluation and appropriate recommendations. The brochure briefly summarizes the role of audiologists and speech language pathologists, and how to find an appropriate certified professional. The contact information for the American Speech Language Hearing Association (ASHA) is provided.

- **Apraxia: A Guide for the Patient and Family**

Source: Stow, OH: Interactive Therapeutics, Inc. 1995. 37 p.

Contact: Available from Interactive Therapeutics, Inc. P.O. Box 1805, Stow, OH 44224. (800) 253-5111 or (216) 688-1371; Fax (330) 923-3030; E-mail: winteract@aol.com. Price: $4.50 each for 1 to 25 copies; bulk rates available.

Summary: This patient education booklet describes apraxia, a disorder involving a disruption in sequencing of voluntary muscle movements; the booklet focuses on the type of apraxia that affects the speech mechanism and makes talking difficult. The booklet presents information in seven chapters: definitions, causes, what it sounds like to have apraxia, other side effects of the disorder, treatment options, self-care and family participation in care, and community support options. The booklet concludes with a glossary and a list of recommended resources for additional reading.

- **Help for Apraxia**

Source: Oceanside, CA: Academic Communication Associates. 1995. 5 p.

Contact: Available from Academic Communication Associates. P.O. Box 586248, Oceanside, CA 92058-6249. (619) 758-9593; Fax (619) 758-1604; E-mail: acom@acadcom.com; http://www.acadcom.com. Price: Single copy free; $13.00 for package of 10 booklets. Item Number 49912-T6.

Summary: This brochure familiarizes readers with apraxia, a neurological communication disorder that is often observed following a stroke or a traumatic brain injury. Individuals with apraxia exhibit speech difficulties in situations where they make conscious, voluntary efforts to produce speech. The author outlines behaviors commonly observed in apraxia and lists guidelines for remediation. The author stresses that words commonly used in the classroom or in the work environment should be emphasized to help the individual communicate effectively in these situations. The brochure concludes with a brief section emphasizing the importance of a team approach in any apraxia treatment program.

- **Traumatic Brain Injury: A Guide for the Patient and Family**

  Source: Stow, OH: Interactive Therapeutics, Inc. 1993. 61 p.

  Contact: Available from Interactive Therapeutics, Inc. P.O. Box 1805, Stow, OH 44224. (800) 253-5111 or (216) 688-1371; Fax (330) 923-3030; E-mail: winteract@aol.com. Price: $4.50 each for 1 to 25 copies; bulk rates available.

  Summary: This booklet is intended to serve as an introduction to traumatic brain injury (TBI) and as a reference to other sources of information to guide patients and their families as they learn about TBI. Four sections cover brain function, TBI and how it affects the brain, what to expect during recovery and rehabilitation, and living and coping with TBI. The chapter on possible impairments from TBI includes a section on speech and language disorders, covering aphasia, communication problems, dysarthria, and apraxia of speech. The booklet concludes with an extensive glossary of terms.

- **Understanding Learning Disabilities**

  Source: Chicago, IL: National Easter Seal Society. 1992. 2 p.

  Contact: Available from National Easter Seal Society. 230 West Monroe Street, Suite 1800, Chicago, IL 60606. Voice (312) 726-6200; TTY (708) 726-4258; Fax (312) 726-1494. Price: $7.50 per 25 copies. Order Number A-240.

  Summary: This brochure provides an overview of learning disabilities and the types of intervention that children with learning disabilities will require. The author stresses that early diagnosis, proper remediation, and the support of caring and informed parents and teachers will do much to help a child with a learning disability overcome the problem. Topics include the incidence of learning disabilities, the signs and symptoms of learning disabilities, strategies for success at home and in the classroom, and likely causes of learning disabilities. The brochure defines three related terms: apraxia, dyslexia, and maturational lag. The brochure is produced by the National Easter Seal Society, an organization founded to help people with disabilities achieve maximum independence.

- **Communication Disorders and HIV: A Guide for Audiologists and Speech-Language Pathologists**

  Source: Rockville, MD: American Speech-Language-Hearing Association (ASHA). 199x. [4 p.].

  Contact: Available from American Speech-Language-Hearing Association (ASHA). Product Sales, 10801 Rockville Pike, Rockville, MD 20852. (888) 498-6699. TTY (301) 897-0157. Website: www.asha.org. Price: Single copy free.

  Summary: This brochure for audiologists and speech language pathologists summarizes the interplay of HIV infection and communication disorders. The author notes that speech, language, and hearing problems frequently result as HIV attacks the central nervous system, with its manifestations occurring in the head and neck. Communication disorders may also occur as a result of treatment options. In many cases, treatments for people with HIV and AIDS and related opportunistic infections rely heavily on drug combinations that are potentially ototoxic. The brochure lists audiologic disorders, including hearing loss, tinnitus, and vertigo; speech language disorders, including aphasia, apraxia, confabulations, dysarthria, dysphagia, confused language, stuttering, and voice disorders; and communication disorders in pediatric AIDS, including elective mutism, hysterical aphonia, and pragmatic language disorder or delay. The brochure concludes with a brief discussion of strategies for treating people with HIV and AIDS, focusing on the professional relationship between client and practitioner, including avoiding prejudice (against lifestyle) and avoiding AIDS-phobia. The author encourages readers to call the ASHA for more information (800-638-8255).

- **Communication Disorders and HIV: The HIV Treatment Community's Guide to Working With Audiologists and Speech Language Pathologists**

  Source: Rockville, MD: American Speech-Language-Hearing Association (ASHA). 199x. [4 p.].

Contact: Available from American Speech-Language-Hearing Association (ASHA). Action Center, 10801 Rockville Pike, Rockville, MD 20852. (800) 638-8255. E-mail: actioncenter@asha.org. Website: www.asha.org. Price: Single copy free for members.

Summary: As people with HIV and AIDS live longer, communication disorders that occur as a direct or indirect consequence of HIV infection are more commonplace. This brochure reviews the communication disorders that may be encountered by people with HIV. Speech, language and hearing problems frequently result as the virus attacks the central nervous system. This brochure is designed to raise awareness of an increasingly significant health problem. The author describes some communication disorders prevalent among people with HIV or AIDS and offers information about the professionals best qualified to treat speech, language or hearing disorders resulting from HIV infection. The brochure covers audiologic disorders, including hearing loss, tinnitus (ringing or other noises in the ears), and vertigo (a spinning form of dizziness); speech and language disorders, including aphasia (loss of the ability to comprehend words), apraxia (loss of ability to carry out complex coordinated movements, can include loss of speech), confabulations (filling in gaps of memory by making things up), dysarthria (difficulty with speech), dysphagia (swallowing difficulty), language of confusion, stuttering, and voice disorders; and communication disorders in children with HIV, including elective mutism (inability to produce speech in specific situations), hysterical aphonia (loss of voice caused by non physical causes), and pragmatic language disorder or delay. The brochure concludes by reminding readers how speech language pathologists are educated and trained to evaluate and treat adults and children with speech, language and swallowing problems.

The National Guideline Clearinghouse™

The National Guideline Clearinghouse™ offers hundreds of evidence-based clinical practice guidelines published in the United States and other countries. You can search their site located at **http://www.guideline.gov** by using the keyword "apraxia" or synonyms.

The NIH Search Utility

After browsing the references listed at the beginning of this chapter, you may want to explore the NIH Search Utility. This allows you to search for documents on over 100 selected Web sites that comprise the NIH-WEB-

SPACE. Each of these servers is "crawled" and indexed on an ongoing basis. Your search will produce a list of various documents, all of which will relate in some way to apraxia. The drawbacks of this approach are that the information is not organized by theme and that the references are often a mix of information for professionals and patients. Nevertheless, a large number of the listed Web sites provide useful background information. We can only recommend this route, therefore, for relatively rare or specific disorders, or when using highly targeted searches. To use the NIH search utility, visit the following Web page: **http://search.nih.gov/index.html**.

NORD (The National Organization of Rare Disorders, Inc.)

NORD provides an invaluable service to the public by publishing, for a nominal fee, short yet comprehensive guidelines on over 1,000 diseases. NORD primarily focuses on rare diseases that might not be covered by the previously listed sources. NORD's Web address is **www.rarediseases.org**. To see if a recent fact sheet has been published on apraxia, simply go to the following hyperlink: **http://www.rarediseases.org/cgi-bin/nord/alphalist**. A complete guide on apraxia can be purchased from NORD for a nominal fee.

Additional Web Sources

A number of Web sites that often link to government sites are available to the public. These can also point you in the direction of essential information. The following is a representative sample:

- AOL: **http://search.aol.com/cat.adp?id=168&layer=&from=subcats**

- drkoop.com®: **http://www.drkoop.com/conditions/ency/index.html**

- Family Village: **http://www.familyvillage.wisc.edu/specific.htm**

- Google:
  http://directory.google.com/Top/Health/Conditions_and_Diseases/

- Med Help International: **http://www.medhelp.org/HealthTopics/A.html**

- Open Directory Project:
  http://dmoz.org/Health/Conditions_and_Diseases/

- Yahoo.com: **http://dir.yahoo.com/Health/Diseases_and_Conditions/**

- WebMD®Health: **http://my.webmd.com/health_topics**

Vocabulary Builder

The material in this chapter may have contained a number of unfamiliar words. The following Vocabulary Builder introduces you to terms used in this chapter that have not been covered in the previous chapter:

Aphasia: Defect or loss of the power of expression by speech, writing, or signs, or of comprehending spoken or written language, due to injury or disease of the brain centres. [EU]

Confusion: Disturbed orientation in regard to time, place, or person, sometimes accompanied by disordered consciousness. [EU]

Dizziness: An imprecise term which may refer to a sense of spatial disorientation, motion of the environment, or lightheadedness. [NIH]

Dysarthria: Imperfect articulation of speech due to disturbances of muscular control which result from damage to the central or peripheral nervous system. [EU]

Dysphagia: Difficulty in swallowing. [EU]

Elective: Subject to the choice or decision of the patient or physician; applied to procedures that are advantageous to the patient but not urgent. [EU]

Gait: Manner or style of walking. [NIH]

Hypotonia: A condition of diminished tone of the skeletal muscles; diminished resistance of muscles to passive stretching. [EU]

Kinetic: Pertaining to or producing motion. [EU]

Laryngectomy: Total or partial excision of the larynx. [NIH]

Larynx: An irregularly shaped, musculocartilaginous tubular structure, lined with mucous membrane, located at the top of the trachea and below the root of the tongue and the hyoid bone. It is the essential sphincter guarding the entrance into the trachea and functioning secondarily as the organ of voice. [NIH]

Lip: Either of the two fleshy, full-blooded margins of the mouth. [NIH]

Mutism: Inability or refusal to speak. [EU]

Neurology: A medical specialty concerned with the study of the structures, functions, and diseases of the nervous system. [NIH]

Oral: Pertaining to the mouth, taken through or applied in the mouth, as an oral medication or an oral thermometer. [EU]

Ototoxic: Having a deleterious effect upon the eighth nerve, or upon the organs of hearing and balance. [EU]

Phobia: A persistent, irrational, intense fear of a specific object, activity, or situation (the phobic stimulus), fear that is recognized as being excessive or unreasonable by the individual himself. When a phobia is a significant source of distress or interferes with social functioning, it is considered a mental disorder; phobic disorder (or neurosis). In DSM III phobic disorders are subclassified as agoraphobia, social phobias, and simple phobias. Used as a word termination denoting irrational fear of or aversion to the subject indicated by the stem to which it is affixed. [EU]

Prejudice: A preconceived judgment made without adequate evidence and not easily alterable by presentation of contrary evidence. [NIH]

Seizures: Clinical or subclinical disturbances of cortical function due to a sudden, abnormal, excessive, and disorganized discharge of brain cells. Clinical manifestations include abnormal motor, sensory and psychic phenomena. Recurrent seizures are usually referred to as epilepsy or "seizure disorder." [NIH]

Symptomatic: 1. pertaining to or of the nature of a symptom. 2. indicative (of a particular disease or disorder). 3. exhibiting the symptoms of a particular disease but having a different cause. 4. directed at the allying of symptoms, as symptomatic treatment. [EU]

Tinnitus: A noise in the ears, as ringing, buzzing, roaring, clicking, etc. Such sounds may at times be heard by others than the patient. [EU]

Tone: 1. the normal degree of vigour and tension; in muscle, the resistance to passive elongation or stretch; tonus. 2. a particular quality of sound or of voice. 3. to make permanent, or to change, the colour of silver stain by chemical treatment, usually with a heavy metal. [EU]

Vertigo: An illusion of movement; a sensation as if the external world were revolving around the patient (objective vertigo) or as if he himself were revolving in space (subjective vertigo). The term is sometimes erroneously used to mean any form of dizziness. [EU]

CHAPTER 2. SEEKING GUIDANCE

Overview

Some patients are comforted by the knowledge that a number of organizations dedicate their resources to helping people with apraxia. These associations can become invaluable sources of information and advice. Many associations offer aftercare support, financial assistance, and other important services. Furthermore, healthcare research has shown that support groups often help people to better cope with their conditions.[8] In addition to support groups, your physician can be a valuable source of guidance and support. Therefore, finding a physician that can work with your unique situation is a very important aspect of your care.

In this chapter, we direct you to resources that can help you find patient organizations and medical specialists. We begin by describing how to find associations and peer groups that can help you better understand and cope with apraxia. The chapter ends with a discussion on how to find a doctor that is right for you.

Associations and Apraxia

As mentioned by the Agency for Healthcare Research and Quality, sometimes the emotional side of an illness can be as taxing as the physical side.[9] You may have fears or feel overwhelmed by your situation. Everyone has different ways of dealing with disease or physical injury. Your attitude, your expectations, and how well you cope with your condition can all

---

[8] Churches, synagogues, and other houses of worship might also have groups that can offer you the social support you need.

[9] This section has been adapted from **http://www.ahcpr.gov/consumer/diaginf5.htm**.

influence your well-being. This is true for both minor conditions and serious illnesses. For example, a study on female breast cancer survivors revealed that women who participated in support groups lived longer and experienced better quality of life when compared with women who did not participate. In the support group, women learned coping skills and had the opportunity to share their feelings with other women in the same situation.

In addition to associations or groups that your doctor might recommend, we suggest that you consider the following list (if there is a fee for an association, you may want to check with your insurance provider to find out if the cost will be covered):

- **March of Dimes Birth Defects Foundation**

    Address: March of Dimes Birth Defects Foundation 1275 Mamaroneck Avenue, White Plains, NY 10605

    Telephone: (914) 428-7100 Toll-free: (888) 663-4637

    Fax: (914) 997-4763

    Email: resourcecenter@modimes.org

    Web Site: http://www.modimes.org

    Background: The March of Dimes Birth Defects Foundation is a national not-for- profit organization that was established in 1938. The mission of the Foundation is to improve the health of babies by preventing birth defects and infant mortality. Through the Campaign for Healthier Babies, the March of Dimes funds programs of research, community services, education, and advocacy. Educational programs that seek to prevent birth defects are important to the Foundation and to that end it produces a wide variety of printed informational materials and videos. The March of Dimes public health educational materials provide information encouraging health- enhancing behaviors that lead to a healthy pregnancy and a healthy baby.

    Relevant area(s) of interest: Huntington's Disease, Myoclonus

- **National Aphasia Association**

    Address: National Aphasia Association 156 Fifth Avenue, Suite 707, New York, NY 10010

    Telephone: (914) 428-7100 Toll-free: (800) 922- 4622

    Fax: (212) 989-7777

    Email: Klein@aphasia.org

    Web Site: http://www.aphasia.org

Background: The National Aphasia Association is a not-for-profit organization dedicated to increasing public awareness of aphasia and other communication disorders and aiding persons with aphasia and their families. Aphasia is a neurological condition caused by damage to the left hemisphere of the brain in which communication and/or language skills (speaking, reading, writing, and comprehending others) are impaired. Established in 1987, the Association's activities include sponsoring support groups, promoting advocacy and legislative programs, supporting ongoing medical research, and maintaining an informational Web site. Other activities include support of a Response Center reachable at (800) 922-4622, publication of a biannual newsletter, sponsorship of biannual national gatherings, and production of fact sheets, reading lists and national listings of community-based support groups, and contact information for a national network of health care professionals who volunteer to respond to families in their area about local resources. A Young People's Network puts families in touch with one another for the purpose of peer support and information exchange.

Relevant area(s) of interest: Apraxia

- **National Eye Research Foundation**

Address: National Eye Research Foundation 910 Skokie Boulevard, Suite 207A, Northbrook, IL 60062

Telephone: (847) 564-4652 Toll-free: (800) 621-2258

Fax: (847) 564-0807

Email: nerf1955@aol.com

Web Site: http://www.nerf.org

Background: The National Eye Research Foundation (NERF) is a nonprofit, international organization dedicated to improving eye care for the public and meeting the professional needs of eye care practitioners. The Foundation sponsors eye research projects on contact lens applications and eye care problems. Established in 1955, NERF is committed to professional enrichment through special study sections in such fields as orthokeratology, primary eye care, pediatrics, and through continuing education programs. The Foundation provides eye care information for the public and professionals. Consisting of 300 members, the organization produces educational materials including a pamphlet series. Program activities include education and referrals. NERF can be reached at its e-mail address at nerf1955ataol.com. or its web site at http://www.nerf.org.

- **Ocular Motor Apraxia Home Page**

Address: Ocular Motor Apraxia Home Page P.O. Box 999, Cambridge, CB1 4WD, United Kingdom

Telephone: 441 223775664

Fax: 441 223775662

Email: oma@wwweb.org

Web Site: http://wwweb.org/oma/

Background: The Ocular Motor Apraxia Home Page is a web site on the Internet dedicated to serving as an information resource on Ocular Motor Apraxia (OMA), a rare visual disorder characterized by absence or impairment of horizontal eye movements. These symptoms may vary from child to child, and may include colic during the first several months; difficulty with horizontal eye movements; head jerks and blinking that help to break focus and then realign focus; and low muscle tone, possibly linked to developmental delay. The OMA Home Page serves as a medical information resource, using the Internet to reach a small and geographically dispersed international audience. The site is dedicated to providing understandable information on OMA, offering online networking opportunities to affected individuals and family members, and promoting research into OMA. The OMA Home Page provides an information leaflet on OMA, a 'What's New' area, and linkage to additional, related sites on the Internet. In addition, the OMA site is compiling a confidential registration database to help determine an accurate count of the occurrence of OMA and to help promote research. The site provides an online registration form where affected individuals and family members can confidentially provide information for inclusion within the database. The OMA Home Page's online networking opportunities include a message board where online visitors may post responses concerning a variety of OMA-related topics; a guestbook where visitors may leave greetings, post messages, ask questions, and/or encourage responses; and a mailing list that enables those with e-mail to discuss any issues relating to OMA. Those who are interested in subscribing to the mailing list may send an e-mail to majordomoatnetlink.co.uk , subject line=anything, body of message='subscribe oma'.

Relevant area(s) of interest: Cogan's Syndrome, Type II

- **Ontario Association for Families of Children with CommunicationDisorders**

  Address: Ontario Association for Families of Children with Communication Disorders 13 Segal Drive, Tillsonburg, Ontario, N4G 4P4, Canada

  Telephone: (519) 842-9506 Toll-free: (800) 922- 4622

  Fax: (519) 842-3228

  Email: oafccd@cyberus.ca

  Web Site: http://www.cyberus.ca/oafccd

  Background: The Ontario Association for Families of Children with Communication Disorders (OAFCCD) is a voluntary self-help organization in Canada that was founded by parents and professionals dedicated to increasing the understanding of communication disorders among parents, program planners, administrators, and the general public. Communication disorders are conditions in which affected individuals have an inability to understand or use speech or language to relate to others in society. Such disorders may be characterized by language, articulation, voice, and/or stuttering abnormalities. Since the OAFCCD was founded in 1994, it has grown to approximately 750 members and 30 chapters. The Association is committed to providing information and support to families of children with communication disorders; assisting families in helping their children access speech and language services; increasing public awareness about the needs of children with such disorders; and promoting awareness of the need for early identification and intervention. In addition, the OAFCCD provides affected families with networking opportunities, conducts local workshops and meetings, sponsors an annual Provincial Conference, and has a web site on the Internet. The Association's educational materials include brochures and a regular newsletter.

  Relevant area(s) of interest: Apraxia

Finding More Associations

There are a number of directories that list additional medical associations that you may find useful. While not all of these directories will provide different information than what is listed above, by consulting all of them, you will have nearly exhausted all sources for patient associations.

The National Health Information Center (NHIC)

The National Health Information Center (NHIC) offers a free referral service to help people find organizations that provide information about apraxia. For more information, see the NHIC's Web site at **http://www.health.gov/NHIC/** or contact an information specialist by calling 1-800-336-4797.

DIRLINE

A comprehensive source of information on associations is the DIRLINE database maintained by the National Library of Medicine. The database comprises some 10,000 records of organizations, research centers, and government institutes and associations which primarily focus on health and biomedicine. DIRLINE is available via the Internet at the following Web site: **http://dirline.nlm.nih.gov/**. Simply type in "apraxia" (or a synonym) or the name of a topic, and the site will list information contained in the database on all relevant organizations.

The Combined Health Information Database

Another comprehensive source of information on healthcare associations is the Combined Health Information Database. Using the "Detailed Search" option, you will need to limit your search to "Organizations" and "apraxia". Type the following hyperlink into your Web browser: **http://chid.nih.gov/detail/detail.html**. To find associations, use the drop boxes at the bottom of the search page where "You may refine your search by." For publication date, select "All Years." Then, select your preferred language and the format option "Organization Resource Sheet." By making these selections and typing in "apraxia" (or synonyms) into the "For these words:" box, you will only receive results on organizations dealing with apraxia. You should check back periodically with this database since it is updated every 3 months.

The National Organization for Rare Disorders, Inc.

The National Organization for Rare Disorders, Inc. has prepared a Web site that provides, at no charge, lists of associations organized by specific diseases. You can access this database at the following Web site: **http://www.rarediseases.org/cgi-bin/nord/searchpage**. Select the option called "Organizational Database (ODB)" and type "apraxia" (or a synonym) in the search box.

Online Support Groups

In addition to support groups, commercial Internet service providers offer forums and chat rooms for people with different illnesses and conditions. WebMD®, for example, offers such a service at their Web site: **http://boards.webmd.com/roundtable**. These online self-help communities can help you connect with a network of people whose concerns are similar to yours. Online support groups are places where people can talk informally. If you read about a novel approach, consult with your doctor or other healthcare providers, as the treatments or discoveries you hear about may not be scientifically proven to be safe and effective.

Finding Doctors

One of the most important aspects of your treatment will be the relationship between you and your doctor or specialist. All patients with apraxia must go through the process of selecting a physician. While this process will vary from person to person, the Agency for Healthcare Research and Quality makes a number of suggestions, including the following:[10]

- If you are in a managed care plan, check the plan's list of doctors first.

- Ask doctors or other health professionals who work with doctors, such as hospital nurses, for referrals.

- Call a hospital's doctor referral service, but keep in mind that these services usually refer you to doctors on staff at that particular hospital. The services do not have information on the quality of care that these doctors provide.

- Some local medical societies offer lists of member doctors. Again, these lists do not have information on the quality of care that these doctors provide.

Additional steps you can take to locate doctors include the following:

- Check with the associations listed earlier in this chapter.

---

[10] This section is adapted from the AHRQ: **www.ahrq.gov/consumer/qntascii/qntdr.htm** .

- Information on doctors in some states is available on the Internet at **http://www.docboard.org**. This Web site is run by "Administrators in Medicine," a group of state medical board directors.

- The American Board of Medical Specialties can tell you if your doctor is board certified. "Certified" means that the doctor has completed a training program in a specialty and has passed an exam, or "board," to assess his or her knowledge, skills, and experience to provide quality patient care in that specialty. Primary care doctors may also be certified as specialists. The AMBS Web site is located at **http://www.abms.org/newsearch.asp**.[11] You can also contact the ABMS by phone at 1-866-ASK-ABMS.

- You can call the American Medical Association (AMA) at 800-665-2882 for information on training, specialties, and board certification for many licensed doctors in the United States. This information also can be found in "Physician Select" at the AMA's Web site: **http://www.ama-assn.org/aps/amahg.htm**.

Finding a Neurologist

The American Academy of Neurology allows you to search for member neurologists by name or location. To use this service, go to **http://www.aan.com/**, select "Find a Neurologist" from the toolbar. Enter your search criteria, and click "Search." To find out more information on a particular neurologist, click on the physician's name.

If the previous sources did not meet your needs, you may want to log on to the Web site of the National Organization for Rare Disorders (NORD) at **http://www.rarediseases.org/**. NORD maintains a database of doctors with expertise in various rare diseases. The Metabolic Information Network (MIN), 800-945-2188, also maintains a database of physicians with expertise in various metabolic diseases.

---

[11] While board certification is a good measure of a doctor's knowledge, it is possible to receive quality care from doctors who are not board certified.

Selecting Your Doctor[2]

When you have compiled a list of prospective doctors, call each of their offices. First, ask if the doctor accepts your health insurance plan and if he or she is taking new patients. If the doctor is not covered by your plan, ask yourself if you are prepared to pay the extra costs. The next step is to schedule a visit with your chosen physician. During the first visit you will have the opportunity to evaluate your doctor and to find out if you feel comfortable with him or her. Ask yourself, did the doctor:

- Give me a chance to ask questions about apraxia?

- Really listen to my questions?

- Answer in terms I understood?

- Show respect for me?

- Ask me questions?

- Make me feel comfortable?

- Address the health problem(s) I came with?

- Ask me my preferences about different kinds of treatments for apraxia?

- Spend enough time with me?

Trust your instincts when deciding if the doctor is right for you. But remember, it might take time for the relationship to develop. It takes more than one visit for you and your doctor to get to know each other.

Working with Your Doctor[3]

Research has shown that patients who have good relationships with their doctors tend to be more satisfied with their care and have better results. Here are some tips to help you and your doctor become partners:

- You know important things about your symptoms and your health history. Tell your doctor what you think he or she needs to know.

- It is important to tell your doctor personal information, even if it makes you feel embarrassed or uncomfortable.

---

[12] This section has been adapted from the AHRQ:
www.ahrq.gov/consumer/qntascii/qntdr.htm.
[13] This section has been adapted from the AHRQ:
www.ahrq.gov/consumer/qntascii/qntdr.htm.

- Bring a "health history" list with you (and keep it up to date).

- Always bring any medications you are currently taking with you to the appointment, or you can bring a list of your medications including dosage and frequency information. Talk about any allergies or reactions you have had to your medications.

- Tell your doctor about any natural or alternative medicines you are taking.

- Bring other medical information, such as x-ray films, test results, and medical records.

- Ask questions. If you don't, your doctor will assume that you understood everything that was said.

- Write down your questions before your visit. List the most important ones first to make sure that they are addressed.

- Consider bringing a friend with you to the appointment to help you ask questions. This person can also help you understand and/or remember the answers.

- Ask your doctor to draw pictures if you think that this would help you understand.

- Take notes. Some doctors do not mind if you bring a tape recorder to help you remember things, but always ask first.

- Let your doctor know if you need more time. If there is not time that day, perhaps you can speak to a nurse or physician assistant on staff or schedule a telephone appointment.

- Take information home. Ask for written instructions. Your doctor may also have brochures and audio and videotapes that can help you.

- After leaving the doctor's office, take responsibility for your care. If you have questions, call. If your symptoms get worse or if you have problems with your medication, call. If you had tests and do not hear from your doctor, call for your test results. If your doctor recommended that you have certain tests, schedule an appointment to get them done. If your doctor said you should see an additional specialist, make an appointment.

By following these steps, you will enhance the relationship you will have with your physician.

Broader Health-Related Resources

In addition to the references above, the NIH has set up guidance Web sites that can help patients find healthcare professionals. These include:[14]

- Caregivers:
  http://www.nlm.nih.gov/medlineplus/caregivers.html

- Choosing a Doctor or Healthcare Service:
  http://www.nlm.nih.gov/medlineplus/choosingadoctororhealthcareserv ice.html

- Hospitals and Health Facilities:
  http://www.nlm.nih.gov/medlineplus/healthfacilities.html

Vocabulary Builder

The following vocabulary builder provides definitions of words used in this chapter that have not been defined in previous chapters:

Blinking: Brief closing of the eyelids by involuntary normal periodic closing, as a protective measure, or by voluntary action. [NIH]

Colic: Paroxysms of pain. This condition usually occurs in the abdominal region but may occur in other body regions as well. [NIH]

Ocular: 1. of, pertaining to, or affecting the eye. 2. eyepiece. [EU]

Pediatrics: A medical specialty concerned with maintaining health and providing medical care to children from birth to adolescence. [NIH]

---

[14] You can access this information at:
http://www.nlm.nih.gov/medlineplus/healthsystem.html.

CHAPTER 3. CLINICAL TRIALS AND APRAXIA

Overview

Very few medical conditions have a single treatment. The basic treatment guidelines that your physician has discussed with you, or those that you have found using the techniques discussed in Chapter 1, may provide you with all that you will require. For some patients, current treatments can be enhanced with new or innovative techniques currently under investigation. In this chapter, we will describe how clinical trials work and show you how to keep informed of trials concerning apraxia.

What Is a Clinical Trial?[15]

Clinical trials involve the participation of people in medical research. Most medical research begins with studies in test tubes and on animals. Treatments that show promise in these early studies may then be tried with people. The only sure way to find out whether a new treatment is safe, effective, and better than other treatments for apraxia is to try it on patients in a clinical trial.

---

[15] The discussion in this chapter has been adapted from the NIH and the NEI: **www.nei.nih.gov/netrials/ctivr.htm**.

What Kinds of Clinical Trials Are There?

Clinical trials are carried out in three phases:

- **Phase I.** Researchers first conduct Phase I trials with small numbers of patients and healthy volunteers. If the new treatment is a medication, researchers also try to determine how much of it can be given safely.

- **Phase II.** Researchers conduct Phase II trials in small numbers of patients to find out the effect of a new treatment on apraxia.

- **Phase III.** Finally, researchers conduct Phase III trials to find out how new treatments for apraxia compare with standard treatments already being used. Phase III trials also help to determine if new treatments have any side effects. These trials--which may involve hundreds, perhaps thousands, of people--can also compare new treatments with no treatment.

How Is a Clinical Trial Conducted?

Various organizations support clinical trials at medical centers, hospitals, universities, and doctors' offices across the United States. The "principal investigator" is the researcher in charge of the study at each facility participating in the clinical trial. Most clinical trial researchers are medical doctors, academic researchers, and specialists. The "clinic coordinator" knows all about how the study works and makes all the arrangements for your visits.

All doctors and researchers who take part in the study on apraxia carefully follow a detailed treatment plan called a protocol. This plan fully explains how the doctors will treat you in the study. The "protocol" ensures that all patients are treated in the same way, no matter where they receive care.

Clinical trials are controlled. This means that researchers compare the effects of the new treatment with those of the standard treatment. In some cases, when no standard treatment exists, the new treatment is compared with no treatment. Patients who receive the new treatment are in the treatment group. Patients who receive a standard treatment or no treatment are in the "control" group. In some clinical trials, patients in the treatment group get a new medication while those in the control group get a placebo. A placebo is a harmless substance, a "dummy" pill, that has no effect on apraxia. In other clinical trials, where a new surgery or device (not a medicine) is being tested, patients in the control group may receive a "sham treatment." This treatment, like a placebo, has no effect on apraxia and does not harm patients.

Researchers assign patients "randomly" to the treatment or control group. This is like flipping a coin to decide which patients are in each group. If you choose to participate in a clinical trial, you will not know which group you will be appointed to. The chance of any patient getting the new treatment is about 50 percent. You cannot request to receive the new treatment instead of the placebo or sham treatment. Often, you will not know until the study is over whether you have been in the treatment group or the control group. This is called a "masked" study. In some trials, neither doctors nor patients know who is getting which treatment. This is called a "double masked" study. These types of trials help to ensure that the perceptions of the patients or doctors will not affect the study results.

Natural History Studies

Unlike clinical trials in which patient volunteers may receive new treatments, natural history studies provide important information to researchers on how apraxia develops over time. A natural history study follows patient volunteers to see how factors such as age, sex, race, or family history might make some people more or less at risk for apraxia. A natural history study may also tell researchers if diet, lifestyle, or occupation affects how a disease or disorder develops and progresses. Results from these studies provide information that helps answer questions such as: How fast will a disease or disorder usually progress? How bad will the condition become? Will treatment be needed?

What Is Expected of Patients in a Clinical Trial?

Not everyone can take part in a clinical trial for a specific disease or disorder. Each study enrolls patients with certain features or eligibility criteria. These criteria may include the type and stage of disease or disorder, as well as, the age and previous treatment history of the patient. You or your doctor can contact the sponsoring organization to find out more about specific clinical trials and their eligibility criteria. If you are interested in joining a clinical trial, your doctor must contact one of the trial's investigators and provide details about your diagnosis and medical history.

If you participate in a clinical trial, you may be required to have a number of medical tests. You may also need to take medications and/or undergo surgery. Depending upon the treatment and the examination procedure, you may be required to receive inpatient hospital care. Or, you may have to return to the medical facility for follow-up examinations. These exams help find out how well the treatment is working. Follow-up studies can take months or years. However, the success of the clinical trial often depends on learning what happens to patients over a long period of time. Only patients who continue to return for follow-up examinations can provide this important long-term information.

Recent Trials on Apraxia

The National Institutes of Health and other organizations sponsor trials on various diseases and disorders. Because funding for research goes to the medical areas that show promising research opportunities, it is not possible for the NIH or others to sponsor clinical trials for every disease and disorder at all times. The following lists recent trials dedicated to apraxia.[16] If the trial listed by the NIH is still recruiting, you may be eligible. If it is no longer recruiting or has been completed, then you can contact the sponsors to learn more about the study and, if published, the results. Further information on the trial is available at the Web site indicated. Please note that some trials may no longer be recruiting patients or are otherwise closed. Before contacting sponsors of a clinical trial, consult with your physician who can help you determine if you might benefit from participation.

- **EEG and EMG Analysis of Ideomotor Apraxia**

    Condition(s): Ideomotor Apraxia

    Study Status: This study is currently recruiting patients.

    Sponsor(s): National Institute of Neurological Disorders and Stroke (NINDS)

    Purpose - Excerpt: This study will examine how the brain operates during execution and control of voluntary movement and what goes wrong with these processes in disease. It will use electroencephalography (EEG) and electromyography (EMG) to compare brain function in normal subjects and in patients with-a disorder affecting patients with stroke and other brain lesions. These patients have problems with timing, sequence and spatial organization of certain types of movements. EEG measures the electrical activity of the brain. The activity is recorded using wire electrodes attached to the scalp or mounted on a Lycra cap placed on the head. EMG measures electrical activity from muscles. It uses wire electrodes placed on the skin over the muscles. Adult healthy normal

---

[16] These are listed at **www.ClinicalTrials.gov**.

volunteers and patients with ideomotor apraxia with a single left brain lesion may be eligible for this study. Study participants will be asked to make certain movements with their arms or hands, such as waving and using scissors. Brain and muscle activity will be measured during these tasks with EEG and EMG recordings. Patients may be asked to repeat these tests over time as their condition changes (such as during recovery from a stroke) to gain information about the recovery process.

Study Type: Observational

Contact(s): Maryland; National Institute of Neurological Disorders and Stroke (NINDS), 9000 Rockville Pike Bethesda, Maryland, 20892, United States; Recruiting; Patient Recruitment and Public Liaison Office 1-800-411-1222 prpl@mail.cc.nih.gov; TTY 1-866-411-1010

Web Site:
http://clinicaltrials.gov/ct/gui/show/NCT00024999;jsessionid=45733F1 0F37D281C9CB2E9D0F1F6C6FC

Benefits and Risks[17]

What Are the Benefits of Participating in a Clinical Trial?

If you are interested in a clinical trial, it is important to realize that your participation can bring many benefits to you and society at large:

- A new treatment could be more effective than the current treatment for apraxia. Although only half of the participants in a clinical trial receive the experimental treatment, if the new treatment is proved to be more effective and safer than the current treatment, then those patients who did not receive the new treatment during the clinical trial may be among the first to benefit from it when the study is over.

- If the treatment is effective, then it may improve health or prevent diseases or disorders.

- Clinical trial patients receive the highest quality of medical care. Experts watch them closely during the study and may continue to follow them after the study is over.

---

[17] This section has been adapted from ClinicalTrials.gov, a service of the National Institutes of Health:
http://www.clinicaltrials.gov/ct/gui/c/a1r/info/whatis?JServSessionIdzone_ct=9jmun6f291.

- People who take part in trials contribute to scientific discoveries that may help other people with apraxia. In cases where certain diseases or disorders run in families, your participation may lead to better care or prevention for your family members.

The Informed Consent

Once you agree to take part in a clinical trial, you will be asked to sign an "informed consent." This document explains a clinical trial's risks and benefits, the researcher's expectations of you, and your rights as a patient.

What Are the Risks?

Clinical trials may involve risks as well as benefits. Whether or not a new treatment will work cannot be known ahead of time. There is always a chance that a new treatment may not work better than a standard treatment. There is also the possibility that it may be harmful. The treatment you receive may cause side effects that are serious enough to require medical attention.

How Is Patient Safety Protected?

Clinical trials can raise fears of the unknown. Understanding the safeguards that protect patients can ease some of these fears. Before a clinical trial begins, researchers must get approval from their hospital's Institutional Review Board (IRB), an advisory group that makes sure a clinical trial is designed to protect patient safety. During a clinical trial, doctors will closely watch you to see if the treatment is working and if you are experiencing any side effects. All the results are carefully recorded and reviewed. In many cases, experts from the Data and Safety Monitoring Committee carefully monitor each clinical trial and can recommend that a study be stopped at any time. You will only be asked to take part in a clinical trial as a volunteer giving informed consent.

What Are a Patient's Rights in a Clinical Trial?

If you are eligible for a clinical trial, you will be given information to help you decide whether or not you want to participate. As a patient, you have the right to:

- Information on all known risks and benefits of the treatments in the study.

- Know how the researchers plan to carry out the study, for how long, and where.

- Know what is expected of you.

- Know any costs involved for you or your insurance provider.

- Know before any of your medical or personal information is shared with other researchers involved in the clinical trial.

- Talk openly with doctors and ask any questions.

After you join a clinical trial, you have the right to:

- Leave the study at any time. Participation is strictly voluntary. However, you should not enroll if you do not plan to complete the study.

- Receive any new information about the new treatment.

- Continue to ask questions and get answers.

- Maintain your privacy. Your name will not appear in any reports based on the study.

- Know whether you participated in the treatment group or the control group (once the study has been completed).

What about Costs?

In some clinical trials, the research facility pays for treatment costs and other associated expenses. You or your insurance provider may have to pay for costs that are considered standard care. These things may include inpatient hospital care, laboratory and other tests, and medical procedures. You also may need to pay for travel between your home and the clinic. You should find out about costs before committing to participation in the trial. If you have health insurance, find out exactly what it will cover. If you don't have health insurance, or if your insurance company will not cover your costs, talk to the clinic staff about other options for covering the cost of your care.

What Should You Ask before Deciding to Join a Clinical Trial?

Questions you should ask when thinking about joining a clinical trial include the following:

- What is the purpose of the clinical trial?

- What are the standard treatments for apraxia? Why do researchers think the new treatment may be better? What is likely to happen to me with or without the new treatment?

- What tests and treatments will I need? Will I need surgery? Medication? Hospitalization?

- How long will the treatment last? How often will I have to come back for follow-up exams?

- What are the treatment's possible benefits to my condition? What are the short- and long-term risks? What are the possible side effects?

- Will the treatment be uncomfortable? Will it make me feel sick? If so, for how long?

- How will my health be monitored?

- Where will I need to go for the clinical trial? How will I get there?

- How much will it cost to be in the study? What costs are covered by the study? How much will my health insurance cover?

- Will I be able to see my own doctor? Who will be in charge of my care?

- Will taking part in the study affect my daily life? Do I have time to participate?

- How do I feel about taking part in a clinical trial? Are there family members or friends who may benefit from my contributions to new medical knowledge?

Keeping Current on Clinical Trials

Various government agencies maintain databases on trials. The U.S. National Institutes of Health, through the National Library of Medicine, has developed ClinicalTrials.gov to provide patients, family members, and physicians with current information about clinical research across the broadest number of diseases and conditions.

The site was launched in February 2000 and currently contains approximately 5,700 clinical studies in over 59,000 locations worldwide, with most studies being conducted in the United States. ClinicalTrials.gov receives about 2 million hits per month and hosts approximately 5,400 visitors daily. To access this database, simply go to their Web site (**www.clinicaltrials.gov**) and search by "apraxia" (or synonyms).

While ClinicalTrials.gov is the most comprehensive listing of NIH-supported clinical trials available, not all trials are in the database. The database is updated regularly, so clinical trials are continually being added. The following is a list of specialty databases affiliated with the National Institutes of Health that offer additional information on trials:

- For clinical studies at the Warren Grant Magnuson Clinical Center located in Bethesda, Maryland, visit their Web site:
  http://clinicalstudies.info.nih.gov/

- For clinical studies conducted at the Bayview Campus in Baltimore, Maryland, visit their Web site:
  http://www.jhbmc.jhu.edu/studies/index.html

- For trials on neurological disorders and stroke, visit and search the Web site sponsored by the National Institute of Neurological Disorders and Stroke of the NIH:
  http://www.ninds.nih.gov/funding/funding_opportunities.htm#Clinica l_Trials

General References

The following references describe clinical trials and experimental medical research. They have been selected to ensure that they are likely to be available from your local or online bookseller or university medical library. These references are usually written for healthcare professionals, so you may consider consulting with a librarian or bookseller who might recommend a particular reference. The following includes some of the most readily available references (sorted alphabetically by title; hyperlinks provide rankings, information and reviews at Amazon.com):

- **A Guide to Patient Recruitment : Today's Best Practices & Proven Strategies** by Diana L. Anderson; Paperback - 350 pages (2001), CenterWatch, Inc.; ISBN: 1930624115;
  http://www.amazon.com/exec/obidos/ASIN/1930624115/icongroupinterna

- **A Step-By-Step Guide to Clinical Trials** by Marilyn Mulay, R.N., M.S., OCN; Spiral-bound - 143 pages Spiral edition (2001), Jones & Bartlett Pub; ISBN: 0763715697;
  http://www.amazon.com/exec/obidos/ASIN/0763715697/icongroupinterna

- **The CenterWatch Directory of Drugs in Clinical Trials** by CenterWatch; Paperback - 656 pages (2000), CenterWatch, Inc.; ISBN: 0967302935; http://www.amazon.com/exec/obidos/ASIN/0967302935/icongroupinterna

- **The Complete Guide to Informed Consent in Clinical Trials** by Terry Hartnett (Editor); Paperback - 164 pages (2000), PharmSource Information Services, Inc.; ISBN: 0970153309; http://www.amazon.com/exec/obidos/ASIN/0970153309/icongroupinterna

- **Dictionary for Clinical Trials** by Simon Day; Paperback - 228 pages (1999), John Wiley & Sons; ISBN: 0471985961; http://www.amazon.com/exec/obidos/ASIN/0471985961/icongroupinterna

- **Extending Medicare Reimbursement in Clinical Trials** by Institute of Medicine Staff (Editor), et al; Paperback 1st edition (2000), National Academy Press; ISBN: 0309068886; http://www.amazon.com/exec/obidos/ASIN/0309068886/icongroupinterna

- **Handbook of Clinical Trials** by Marcus Flather (Editor); Paperback (2001), Remedica Pub Ltd; ISBN: 1901346293; http://www.amazon.com/exec/obidos/ASIN/1901346293/icongroupinterna

Vocabulary Builder

The following vocabulary builder gives definitions of words used in this chapter that have not been defined in previous chapters:

Electroencephalography: The recording of the electric currents developed in the brain, by means of electrodes applied to the scalp, to the surface of the brain (intracranial e.) or placed within the substance of the brain (depth e.). [EU]

Electromyography: Recording of the changes in electric potential of muscle by means of surface or needle electrodes. [NIH]

Lesion: Any pathological or traumatic discontinuity of tissue or loss of function of a part. [EU]

PART II: ADDITIONAL RESOURCES AND ADVANCED MATERIAL

ABOUT PART II

In Part II, we introduce you to additional resources and advanced research on apraxia. All too often, patients who conduct their own research are overwhelmed by the difficulty in finding and organizing information. The purpose of the following chapters is to provide you an organized and structured format to help you find additional information resources on apraxia. In Part II, as in Part I, our objective is not to interpret the latest advances on apraxia or render an opinion. Rather, our goal is to give you access to original research and to increase your awareness of sources you may not have already considered. In this way, you will come across the advanced materials often referred to in pamphlets, books, or other general works. Once again, some of this material is technical in nature, so consultation with a professional familiar with apraxia is suggested.

CHAPTER 4. STUDIES ON APRAXIA

Overview

Every year, academic studies are published on apraxia or related conditions. Broadly speaking, there are two types of studies. The first are peer reviewed. Generally, the content of these studies has been reviewed by scientists or physicians. Peer-reviewed studies are typically published in scientific journals and are usually available at medical libraries. The second type of studies is non-peer reviewed. These works include summary articles that do not use or report scientific results. These often appear in the popular press, newsletters, or similar periodicals.

In this chapter, we will show you how to locate peer-reviewed references and studies on apraxia. We will begin by discussing research that has been summarized and is free to view by the public via the Internet. We then show you how to generate a bibliography on apraxia and teach you how to keep current on new studies as they are published or undertaken by the scientific community.

The Combined Health Information Database

The Combined Health Information Database summarizes studies across numerous federal agencies. To limit your investigation to research studies and apraxia, you will need to use the advanced search options. First, go to **http://chid.nih.gov/index.html**. From there, select the "Detailed Search" option (or go directly to that page with the following hyperlink: **http://chid.nih.gov/detail/detail.html**). The trick in extracting studies is found in the drop boxes at the bottom of the search page where "You may refine your search by." Select the dates and language you prefer, and the format option "Journal Article." At the top of the search form, select the number of records you would like to see (we recommend 100) and check the box to display "whole records." We recommend that you type in "apraxia" (or synonyms) into the "For these words:" box. Consider using the option "anywhere in record" to make your search as broad as possible. If you want to limit the search to only a particular field, such as the title of the journal, then select this option in the "Search in these fields" drop box. The following is a sample of what you can expect from this type of search:

- **Motor Apraxia in Dementia**

  Source: Perceptual and Motor Skills. 79(1 Part 2): 523-528. August 1994.

  Summary: This study assessed motor apraxia in 25 patients with presumed dementia of the Alzheimer type and 23 patients with presumed multi-infarct dementia. Apraxia was assessed using a test in which the patient is required to carry out five actions in each of four categories: facial (e.g., whistle), upper limb intransitive (e.g., wave goodbye), transitive (e.g., pretend to use a spoon to eat), and complex (e.g., pretend to light a cigarette). Findings suggest that apraxia was common in both groups and was usually only mild. It correlated most strongly with language-related impairments in the Alzheimer group, as has been found in other patient groups, whereas in the group with multi-infarct dementia the pattern of correlation was less clear. It was not strongly related to performance on tests involving constructional praxis or to age in either group. Implications of the findings for clinical assessment are noted. 2 tables, 14 references. (AA-M).

- **Development of Aphasia, Apraxia, and Agnosia and Decline in Alzheimer's Disease**

  Source: American Journal of Psychiatry. 150(5): 742-747. May 1993.

  Summary: This case series study examined whether the rate of clinical decline varied among persons with Alzheimer's disease who showed early development of aphasia (dysfunction in using language), apraxia (dysfunction in ability to carry out actions), and/or agnosia (dysfunction in recognizing what should be familiar). Study participants were administered the Mini-Mental State Examination (MMSE) every 6-12 months; each participant was assessed at least three times. Results showed that participants who developed aphasia and apraxia declined more rapidly on the MMSE than those who did not. These results suggest that Alzheimer's disease does not progress through a series of stages. Rather, they support the notion that there are distinct subtypes of Alzheimer's disease, each of which may have its own pattern of decline.

In this case, it seems that accelerated decline is associated with the relatively early onset of certain neurological signs. 22 references.

- **Constructional Apraxia in Alzheimer's Disease: Contributions to Functional Loss**

Source: Physical and Occupational Therapy in Geriatrics. 9(3): 53-68. Spring 1991.

Contact: Available from Haworth Press, Inc. 10 Alice Street, Binghamton, NY 13904. (800) 3-HAWORTH. Price: Call for information.

Summary: This article describes a study that examined the relationship of constructional apraxia to the performance of activities of daily living through the stages of Alzheimer's disease. According to the authors, the nature and assessment of constructional apraxia, or difficulty in assembling one-dimensional units into two-dimensional patterns or figures, is currently being debated. Numerous studies into the measurement of constructional apraxia, its causes, and how it influences the performance of daily living activities are cited and discussed. This study consisted of assessments of the following groups of individuals: 113 people without dementia; 27 people with questionable dementia; 34 people with mild dementia; 29 people with moderate dementia; and 52 people with severe dementia. Results from data obtained through the constructional apraxia test items, an assessment of the caregiver's perception of the patient's functional capacity, language function tests of the patients, and a memory assessment using the Short Portable Mental Status Questionnaire showed that constructional deficits increased as dementia progressed. Of the activities of daily living tasks, dressing performance was slightly more impaired than the others. The authors assert that the results of this study demonstrate that constructional deficits exist in some patients during the early stages of Alzheimer's disease, and that these findings indicate the need for early assessment and intervention to help the patient and his or her family address functional loss. 30 references.

- **Meeting the Challenge of Suspected Developmental Apraxia of Speech Through Inclusion**

Source: Topics in Language Disorders. 19:(3): 19-35. May 1999.

Contact: Available from Aspen Publishers, Inc. 7201 McKinney Circle, Frederick, MD 21704. (800) 234-1660. Website: www.aspenpublishers.com.

Summary: This article proposes an inclusion classroom as a service delivery model for children with severe intelligibility problems (often diagnosed as developmental apraxia of speech or DAS). This full day, year round kindergarten classroom was developed through a partnership involving university faculty and school district personnel interested in the assessment and treatment options for these children. The classroom is unique in that it pairs children with phonological disorders with individuals who have speech and language behaviors that are typically developing. In addition, a speech language pathologist is teamed with a regular kindergarten teacher for instructional purposes. Academic information is presented along with activities designed to improve speech production capabilities. The authors first discuss clinical issues associated with identifying and treating DAS. The authors then identify aspects of program development, including the successes and areas for improvement noted in their own classroom experience. 4 figures. 33 references. (AA).

- **Developmental Apraxia of Speech: I. Descriptive and Theoretical Perspectives**

Source: Journal of Speech, Language, and Hearing Research. 40(2): 273-285. April 1997.

Summary: This article reviews descriptive and theoretical perspectives related to the developmental apraxia of speech (DAS). DAS is a putative diagnostic category for children whose speech errors presumably differ from the errors of children with developmental speech delay (SD) and resemble the errors of adults with acquired apraxia of speech. The studies reported in this series concern both premises, with primary focus on the first: that children with DAS can be differentiated from children with SD on the basis of one or more reliable differences in their speech error profiles. Immediate goals are to identify a diagnostic marker for DAS and to consider implications for research and clinical practice. A long-term goal is to identify the phenotype marker for DAS, on the assumption that it may be a genetically transmitted disorder. 1 figure. 1 table. 89 references. (AA-M).

- **Developmental Apraxia of Speech: III. A Subtype Marked by Inappropriate Stress**

Source: Journal of Speech, Language, and Hearing Research. 40(2): 313-337. April 1997.

Summary: This article reports on a study of developmental apraxia of speech (DAS), focusing on a subtype marked by inappropriate stress. This study, the third in a series, is of particular interest because it cross-validates the prior stress findings. The studies use conversational speech samples from 19 children with suspected DAS, provided by five DAS researchers at geographically diverse diagnostic facilities in North America. Summed across the three studies, 52 percent of 48 eligible samples from 53 children with suspected DAS had inappropriate stress, compared to 10 percent of 71 eligible samples from 73 age-matched children with speech delay of unknown origin. The authors first discuss the implications of these stress findings for theories of the origin and nature of DAS. Perspectives in psycholinguistics, neurolinguistics, and developmental biolinguistics lead to five working hypotheses pending validation in ongoing studies. The five hypotheses are: inappropriate stress is a diagnostic marker for at least one subtype of DAS; the psycholinguistic loci of inappropriate stress in this subtype of DAS are in the phonological representational process; the proximal origin of this subtype of DAS is a neurogenically specific deficit; the distal origin of this form of DAS is an inherited genetic polymorphism; and significant differences between acquired apraxia of speech in adults and findings for this subtype of DAS call into question the inference that it is an apractic, motor speech disorder. The authors conclude with a discussion of the implications of these findings for research and clinical practice in DAS. 2 figures. 4 tables. 127 references. (AA-M).

- **Vocal Apraxia: Identification Contributes to Rehabilitation of Whole Person**

Source: Advance for Speech Pathologists and Audiologists. 5(25): 8, 17. June 26, 1995.

Contact: Available from Merion Publications, Inc. 650 Park Avenue, Box 61556, King of Prussia, PA 19406-0956. (800) 355-1088 or (610) 265-7812.

Summary: This article, from a professional newsletter for speech-language pathologists and audiologists, discusses rehabilitation of patients with vocal apraxia. The article consists primarily of an interview with Tish Moody, a private speech language therapist. Moody defines the core characteristics of vocal apraxia as asynchronic respiratory-phonatory responses, disruption of vocalization, and the inability to initiate vocalization. The article covers the incidence and prevalence of this condition, particularly in patients with stroke or traumatic brain injury (TBI); etiologic considerations; clinical presentation and diagnostic issues; and treatment options for stimulating vocal productivity in individuals with the disorder. Skill areas discussed include: initiation of vocalization; respiration for phonation and sustained vocalization; pitch range control and prosody; volume control; and quality and resonance. The article concludes with Moody's address and telephone number.

Federally-Funded Research on Apraxia

The U.S. Government supports a variety of research studies relating to apraxia and associated conditions. These studies are tracked by the Office of Extramural Research at the National Institutes of Health.[18] CRISP (Computerized Retrieval of Information on Scientific Projects) is a searchable database of federally-funded biomedical research projects conducted at universities, hospitals, and other institutions. Visit the CRISP Web site at **http://commons.cit.nih.gov/crisp3/CRISP.Generate_Ticket**.   You   can perform targeted searches by various criteria including geography, date, as well as topics related to apraxia and related conditions.

For most of the studies, the agencies reporting into CRISP provide summaries or abstracts. As opposed to clinical trial research using patients, many federally-funded studies use animals or simulated models to explore apraxia and related conditions. In some cases, therefore, it may be difficult to understand how some basic or fundamental research could eventually translate into medical practice. The following sample is typical of the type of information found when searching the CRISP database for apraxia:

- **Project Title: Genetic Studies of Apraxia and Speech Sound Disorders**

  Principal Investigator & Institution: Iyengar, Sudha K.; Associate Professor; Epidemiology and Biostatistics; Case Western Reserve University 10900 Euclid Ave Cleveland, Oh 44106

  Timing: Fiscal Year 2000; Project Start 5-JAN-1999; Project End 1-DEC-2001

  Summary: This is a pilot grant to examine the familial and genetic basis of developmental phonology disorders, the most prevalent group of communication disorders in children. The overall goal of this project is to determine if a gene(s) on chromosome 7q31 plays a substantial role in development of phonology disorders in the general population. We will examine ten microsatellite markers encompassing a 5.6 cM region on chromosome 7q31 in 20 families of children with Developmental Apraxia of Speech (DAS) and 20 families of children with developmental phonology disorders identified in a familial study of phonology disorders. A recent study of a single family with DAS in combination with a grammatical deficit found linkage of this phenotype to markers on

---

[18] Healthcare projects are funded by the National Institutes of Health (NIH), Substance Abuse and Mental Health Services (SAMHSA), Health Resources and Services Administration (HRSA), Food and Drug Administration (FDA), Centers for Disease Control and Prevention (CDCP), Agency for Healthcare Research and Quality (AHRQ), and Office of Assistant Secretary of Health (OASH).

this 5.6 cM region of chromosome 7q31. This study was the first clear demonstration that susceptibility to speech sound disorders is mediated via genes. We intend to extend these analyses to a more substantive dataset from the general population to determine if the locus on chromosome 7 has a substantial impact in the etiology of developmental phonology disorders. Model-free approaches to genetic linkage analysis based upon juvenile sibling pairs concordant for DAS or developmental phonology disorder will be used to evaluate phenotypic data separately and as a composite. We will use linkage disequilibrium analysis for fine mapping if we obtain evidence for linkage. Family-based association testing methods will be used to evaluate if any of the markers tested are in very close proximity to the gene for apraxia. This application is intended to provide a core for a further, more extensive, acquisition of DAS and developmental phonology disorder phenotype and genotype data. We, ultimately, intend to expand the entire population to include a genome scan and to positionally clone genes for developmental phonology disorders.

Website: http://commons.cit.nih.gov/crisp3/CRISP.Generate_Ticket

- **Project Title: Articulatory and Perceptual Correlates of Syllable Structure**

Principal Investigator & Institution: De Jong, Kenneth J.; Linguistics; Indiana University Bloomington Bryan Hall Bloomington, in 47405

Timing: Fiscal Year 2000; Project Start 1-SEP-2000; Project End 1-AUG-2003

Summary: This proposal describes research which will determine articulatory, acoustic and perceptual correlates of the basic syllabic types in English speech production. This research also provides the basis for future research which will determine the factors which contribute to the appearance of syllabic organization in speech. Two projects are described which employ an elicitation paradigm in which speakers repeat tokens of various syllable structures in time to a metronome. Each experiment, then, examines the effect of producing sequences at different rates. A pilot study has revealed that each syllable type is characterized by stability in various temporal aspects across an extreme variety of rates. Also the pilot reveals modality shifts which occur as speakers change rates. The first proposed project will analyze a previously acquired set of articulatory data which includes articulatory motion in the sagittal plane as well as an indicator of the time course of glottal opening. These articulatory records will be analyzed for correlates of basic syllable structures, as well as for gradient and sudden changes in temporal organization due to rate changes. Such analyses will reveal aspects of gestural timing which remain stable for a particular syllable structure, and which are subject to systematic rate variation. In the second project, acoustic records will be submitted to perceptual analyses in order to determine which aspects of the articulation and acoustics are used by listeners in identifying a syllabic type. In this manner, perceptual correlates of syllable structure will also be obtained. The research proposed here will provide a definitive characterization of the temporal structure of basic syllable types, as well as provide a foundation for determining what factors in production and perception give rise to syllabic structure in speech in general. The findings of this project will thus be important for advances in research in speech production, speech apraxia, language acquisition and linguistics.

Website: http://commons.cit.nih.gov/crisp3/CRISP.Generate_Ticket

- **Project Title: Core--Clinical**

Principal Investigator & Institution: Doody, Rachelle; Baylor College of Medicine 1 Baylor Plaza Houston, Tx 77030

Timing: Fiscal Year 2000

Summary: The Clinical Core recruits, diagnoses, and characterized AD patients and controls for clinical and basic research. We have recruited men and women from minority groups and from rural and urban areas of Texas and surrounding states. We investigate progression, clinical heterogeneity related to hemispheric specialization, and the neuropathologic basis of this clinical heterogeneity which may help to elucidate subtypes and factors which affect decline in Alzheimer's Disease. We desire a representative population and will therefore enroll ethnic minority subjects through a program for professionals who provide care to minorities. We will work closely with the Education and Information Transfer Core to actualize this aim. Clinical, basic science and neuropathologic projects require appropriate controls, so we will continue entering spousal controls, and have also identified a new source for normal elderly controls. We have expanded our procedures for differentiating familial and sporadic AD. We will provide quantitative measurements of progression using a calculated rate of progression and measured progression rates for cognitive and functional deficits. Our study of progression will attend to relative progression of lateralized behavioral and cognitive problems. In order to increase the duration of follow-up, we have developed a comprehensive Telephone Follow-up Program, and a new instrument to gather data about cognitive and behavioral problems by telephone. We will work with Neuropathology Core and Project 3 to examine site specific anatomical changes using plaque ad tangle counts, synaptophysin strains, and measures of inflammation in brain regions hypothesized to account for lateralized cognitive abnormalities, beginning with aphasia and apraxia. We will continue to explore models for cognitive dysfunction in AD, such as the model for semantic memory tested in Pilot Project 1. Finally, we will continue encouraging researchers from the ADRC and broader medical community to utilize our expertise, database, Serum Bank, and consenting patients and controls to advance understanding of Alzheimer's Disease.

Website: http://commons.cit.nih.gov/crisp3/CRISP.Generate_Ticket

- **Project Title: Familial Study of Severe Phonology Disorders**

Principal Investigator & Institution: Lewis, Barbara A.; Associate Professor; Pediatrics; Case Western Reserve University 10900 Euclid Ave Cleveland, Oh 44106

Timing: Fiscal Year 2000; Project Start 1-JAN-1999; Project End 1-DEC-2003

Summary: This project will examine the familial and genetic basis of developmental phonology disorders, the most prevalent group of communication disorders in children. Behavioral and molecular genetic techniques will be used to differentiate clinically based phenotypes of developmental phonology disorders, including phonology disorders in isolation, phonology disorders that are comorbid with other language disorders, and developmental apraxia of speech. A large cohort of sib pairs, N=500, ascertained through a proband with a phonology disorder, will be examined on measures of phonology, expressive and receptive language, speech, and reading. Data analysis, including segregation analyses, will examine family resemblance, sibling correlations, and heritability. Model-free approaches to genetic linkage analysis based upon sibling pairs will be used to evaluate candidate genes that have been associated with phonological processing abilities in studies of reading. Gender differences in phenotypes and modes of transmission of phonology disorders will be examined. Longitudinal follow-up of individuals with histories of preschool phonology disorders will provide data on adolescent outcomes for speech, language, reading, spelling and writing abilities. The overall aim of the project is to improve understanding of genetic basis, behavioral phenotypes, and developmental outcomes of phonology disorders.

Website: http://commons.cit.nih.gov/crisp3/CRISP.Generate_Ticket

- **Project Title: Genetics of Autism and Other Communication Disorders**

Principal Investigator & Institution: Gernsbacher, Morton A.; Professor; Psychology; University of Wisconsin Madison 500 Lincoln Dr Madison, Wi 53706

Timing: Fiscal Year 2001; Project Start 1-SEP-2001

Summary: (provided by applicant): The goal of this research project is to advance rapidly the current genetic research on autism. I suggest that the existing results of genetic (i.e., genome screen) studies have been less definitive because of the heterogeneity among persons with autistic spectrum disorders. Even when diagnosed according to strict and consistent criteria (e.g., the Autism Diagnostic Inventory), symptom profiles of persons with autism vary greatly, suggesting variability in etiology. Thus, I propose to identify and validate a putative subtype of autism, which I refer to as "developmental verbal dyspraxia." Developmental verbal dyspraxia (DVD) is a motor-speech programming disorder resulting in difficulty coordinating and sequencing the oral-motor movements necessary to produce and combine speech sounds (phonemes) to form syllables, words, phrases, and sentences. I hypothesize that a sizable minority of minimally or nonverbal persons with autism are characterized by developmental verbal dyspraxia. Support for my hypothesis comes from behavioral, genetic, and neuroanatomical evidence. In ongoing research (in collaboration with Hill Goldsmith) I am identifying and validating a DVD subtype of autism by screening all children with autism (under age 18) in a metropolitan area; identifying the members of this group who are also characterized by DVD; selecting an autism control group of children not characterized by DVD and a typically developing control group; collecting extensive behavioral, medical, and developmental histories of all children in these groups; obtaining neuroanatomical (structural MRI) data; and collecting and storing DNA. The goal of the research training for this fellowship is to construct indices of the DVD subtype from the diagnostic instruments that have been used in the previously conducted genome screens (e.g., the ADI and A-DOS) and apply those indices to the existing screen data to identify candidate gene regions for the autism-DVD subtype.

Website: http://commons.cit.nih.gov/crisp3/CRISP.Generate_Ticket

- **Project Title: Mental Representations of Goal-Directed Procedures**

Principal Investigator & Institution: Zacks, Jeffrey M.; Psychology; Washington University Lindell and Skinker Blvd St. Louis, Mo 63130

Timing: Fiscal Year 2000; Project Start 1-AUG-2000; Project End 1-JUL-2002

Summary: Normal cognition is characterized by the ability to flexibly learn new procedures and to perform previously learned procedures. When this ability is disturbed, as in frontal apraxia, consequences are profound. Normal procedural learning may depend in part on hierarchically organized representations of the temporal structure of activity. Motivated by a theoretical account of event representations and recent work on the perception of goal-directed tasks, I hypothesize that such representations are shared across perception and skill acquisition. The studies proposed here test this hypothesis using a procedural learning program. Participants will learn a novel everyday procedural task, using a computer-based training system. Varying the layout of the computer interface allows a direct test of the role of the proposed event representations: Layouts that directly represent the temporal organization of the activity are hypothesized to lead to better performance. Varying the medium in which the information is presented (still pictures or video) allows a test of the specificity of these representations. In addition to testing the basic hypothesis, each of the two proposed experiments will examine a secondary theoretical issue. In the first experiment, a test of explicit memory for the task instructions will indicate the degree to which explicit memory mediates understanding of event structure. In the second experiment, a test of task transfer will indicate the degree to which representations of task structure are internalized and flexibly re-used. By taking advantage of a paradigm derived from recent theoretical and empirical work, these experiments will clarify the role of structured representations of events in normal cognition. They also provide a basis to develop systems to help patients cope with impaired procedural knowledge, as well as a basis for systems to assist in skill instruction.

Website: http://commons.cit.nih.gov/crisp3/CRISP.Generate_Ticket

- **Project Title: Organization and Breakdown of Routine Action Skills**

  Principal Investigator & Institution: Schwartz, Myrna F.; Associate Director; Moss Rehabilitation Hospital 1200 W Tabor Rd Philadelphia, Pa 19141

  Timing: Fiscal Year 2001; Project Start 1-APR-1993; Project End 1-JUL-2002

  Summary: (Adapted From The Investigator s Abstract): Neuropsychological theory has it that the occurrence of errors in routine action involving objects is diagnostic of ideational apraxia - a left hemisphere syndrome. A large-scale study conducted under the current grant is showing that vulnerability to action errors exists in both let and right hemisphere strokes and in closed head injury. Moreover, the three patient groups display a similar response to situational complexity and a similar pattern of errors. To elucidate the conditions that bring about action breakdown, a program of single case studies is being conducted. These studies suggest that the status of executive functions is more important than praxis or semantic memory for objects. This continuation grant aims at a better understanding of the necessary and sufficient conditions for routine action breakdown. The formal study of naturalistic action in brain damaged populations and the program of single case studies begun under the current grant will be continued, and two new series of experiments will be undertaken. The first is an exploration of distracter effects in reaching to targets, which bears on the mechanisms underlying objects substitution errors. The second explores whether competing plans or concurrent memory-load manipulations induce action errors in non-neurological subjects and in patients who are vulnerable to attention/working memory deficits. This second series of experiments is motivated by a theory of attention and action proposed by Norman and Shallice. Shallice and colleagues recently developed a computational model that implements aspects of the theory relating to routine action production. Under a subcontract to Shallice's group, this modeling effort will continue and will focus on simulating normal and pathological performance under increasing situational complexity. Finally, having developed methods for assessing naturalistic action production under increasing task demands, we now propose to create a screening tool for use in the clinic and to test its predictive validity against scales of instrumental activities of daily living.

Website: http://commons.cit.nih.gov/crisp3/CRISP.Generate_Ticket

The National Library of Medicine: PubMed

One of the quickest and most comprehensive ways to find academic studies in both English and other languages is to use PubMed, maintained by the National Library of Medicine. The advantage of PubMed over previously mentioned sources is that it covers a greater number of domestic and foreign references. It is also free to the public.[19] If the publisher has a Web site that offers full text of its journals, PubMed will provide links to that site, as well

[19] PubMed was developed by the National Center for Biotechnology Information (NCBI) at the National Library of Medicine (NLM) at the National Institutes of Health (NIH). The PubMed database was developed in conjunction with publishers of biomedical literature as a search tool for accessing literature citations and linking to full-text journal articles at Web sites of participating publishers. Publishers that participate in PubMed supply NLM with their citations electronically prior to or at the time of publication.

as to sites offering other related data. User registration, a subscription fee, or some other type of fee may be required to access the full text of articles in some journals.

To generate your own bibliography of studies dealing with apraxia, simply go to the PubMed Web site at **www.ncbi.nlm.nih.gov/pubmed**. Type "apraxia" (or synonyms) into the search box, and click "Go." The following is the type of output you can expect from PubMed for "apraxia" (hyperlinks lead to article summaries):

- **Singing as therapy for apraxia of speech and aphasia: report of a case.**
  Author(s): Keith RL, Aronson AE.
  Source: Brain and Language. 1975 October; 2(4): 483-8. No Abstract Available.
  http://www.ncbi.nlm.nih.gov:80/entrez/query.fcgi?cmd=Retrieve&db=PubMed&list_uids=1218380&dopt=Abstract

- **Visuoimaginal constructional apraxia: on a case of selective deficit of imagery.**
  Author(s): Grossi D, Orsini A, Modafferi A, Liotti M.
  Source: Brain and Cognition. 1986 July; 5(3): 255-67.
  http://www.ncbi.nlm.nih.gov:80/entrez/query.fcgi?cmd=Retrieve&db=PubMed&list_uids=3756003&dopt=Abstract

Vocabulary Builder

Agnosia: Loss of the ability to comprehend the meaning or recognize the importance of various forms of stimulation that cannot be attributed to impairment of a primary sensory modality. Tactile agnosia is characterized by an inability to perceive the shape and nature of an object by touch alone, despite unimpaired sensation to light touch, position, and other primary sensory modalities. [NIH]

Anatomical: Pertaining to anatomy, or to the structure of the organism. [EU]

Ataxia: Failure of muscular coordination; irregularity of muscular action. [EU]

Atrophy: A wasting away; a diminution in the size of a cell, tissue, organ, or part. [EU]

Auditory: Pertaining to the sense of hearing. [EU]

Bilateral: Having two sides, or pertaining to both sides. [EU]

Blepharitis: Inflammation of the eyelids. [EU]

Blepharospasm: Excessive winking; tonic or clonic spasm of the orbicularis oculi muscle. [NIH]

Cerebral: Of or pertaining of the cerebrum or the brain. [EU]

Cognition: Intellectual or mental process whereby an organism becomes aware of or obtains knowledge. [NIH]

Concomitant: Accompanying; accessory; joined with another. [EU]

Cornea: The transparent structure forming the anterior part of the fibrous tunic of the eye. It consists of five layers : (1) the anterior corneal epithelium, continuous with that of the conjunctiva, (2) the anterior limiting layer (Bowman's membrane), (3) the substantia propria, or stroma, (4) the posterior limiting layer (Descemet's membrane), and (5) the endothelium of the anterior chamber, called also keratoderma. [EU]

Cortex: The outer layer of an organ or other body structure, as distinguished from the internal substance. [EU]

Cortical: Pertaining to or of the nature of a cortex or bark. [EU]

Dementia: An acquired organic mental disorder with loss of intellectual abilities of sufficient severity to interfere with social or occupational functioning. The dysfunction is multifaceted and involves memory, behavior, personality, judgment, attention, spatial relations, language, abstract thought, and other executive functions. The intellectual decline is usually progressive, and initially spares the level of consciousness. [NIH]

Distal: Remote; farther from any point of reference; opposed to proximal. In dentistry, used to designate a position on the dental arch farther from the median line of the jaw. [EU]

Dorsal: 1. pertaining to the back or to any dorsum. 2. denoting a position more toward the back surface than some other object of reference; same as posterior in human anatomy; superior in the anatomy of quadrupeds. [EU]

Enzyme: A protein molecule that catalyses chemical reactions of other substances without itself being destroyed or altered upon completion of the reactions. Enzymes are classified according to the recommendations of the Nomenclature Committee of the International Union of Biochemistry. Each enzyme is assigned a recommended name and an Enzyme Commission (EC) number. They are divided into six main groups; oxidoreductases, transferases, hydrolases, lyases, isomerases, and ligases. [EU]

Genotype: The genetic constitution of the individual; the characterization of the genes. [NIH]

Histidine: An essential amino acid important in a number of metabolic processes. It is required for the production of histamine. [NIH]

Idiopathic: Of the nature of an idiopathy; self-originated; of unknown causation. [EU]

Inflammation: A pathological process characterized by injury or destruction of tissues caused by a variety of cytologic and chemical reactions. It is usually manifested by typical signs of pain, heat, redness, swelling, and loss of function. [NIH]

Keratitis: Inflammation of the cornea. [EU]

Lethal: Deadly, fatal. [EU]

Lobe: A more or less well-defined portion of any organ, especially of the brain, lungs, and glands. Lobes are demarcated by fissures, sulci, connective tissue, and by their shape. [EU]

Microbiology: The study of microorganisms such as fungi, bacteria, algae, archaea, and viruses. [NIH]

Molecular: Of, pertaining to, or composed of molecules : a very small mass of matter. [EU]

Musculature: The muscular apparatus of the body, or of any part of it. [EU]

Neural: 1. pertaining to a nerve or to the nerves. 2. situated in the region of the spinal axis, as the neutral arch. [EU]

Neurons: The basic cellular units of nervous tissue. Each neuron consists of a body, an axon, and dendrites. Their purpose is to receive, conduct, and transmit impulses in the nervous system. [NIH]

Neurophysiology: The scientific discipline concerned with the physiology of the nervous system. [NIH]

Neuropsychology: A branch of psychology which investigates the correlation between experience or behavior and the basic neurophysiological processes. The term neuropsychology stresses the dominant role of the nervous system. It is a more narrowly defined field than physiological psychology or psychophysiology. [NIH]

Parietal: 1. of or pertaining to the walls of a cavity. 2. pertaining to or located near the parietal bone, as the parietal lobe. [EU]

Phenotype: The outward appearance of the individual. It is the product of interactions between genes and between the genotype and the environment. This includes the killer phenotype, characteristic of yeasts. [NIH]

Phonation: The process of producing vocal sounds by means of vocal cords vibrating in an expiratory blast of air. [NIH]

Photophobia: Abnormal visual intolerance of light. [EU]

Polypeptide: A peptide which on hydrolysis yields more than two amino acids; called tripeptides, tetrapeptides, etc. according to the number of amino acids contained. [EU]

Polyphosphates: Linear polymers in which orthophosphate residues are linked with energy-rich phosphoanhydride bonds. They are found in plants, animals, and microorganisms. [NIH]

Posterior: Situated in back of, or in the back part of, or affecting the back or dorsal surface of the body. In lower animals, it refers to the caudal end of the body. [EU]

Prevalence: The total number of cases of a given disease in a specified population at a designated time. It is differentiated from incidence, which refers to the number of new cases in the population at a given time. [NIH]

Progressive: Advancing; going forward; going from bad to worse; increasing in scope or severity. [EU]

Proteins: Polymers of amino acids linked by peptide bonds. The specific sequence of amino acids determines the shape and function of the protein. [NIH]

Proximal: Nearest; closer to any point of reference; opposed to distal. [EU]

Psychiatry: The medical science that deals with the origin, diagnosis, prevention, and treatment of mental disorders. [NIH]

Psychology: The science dealing with the study of mental processes and behavior in man and animals. [NIH]

Retraction: 1. the act of drawing back; the condition of being drawn back. 2. distal movement of teeth, usually accomplished with an orthodontic appliance. [EU]

Serum: The clear portion of any body fluid; the clear fluid moistening serous membranes. 2. blood serum; the clear liquid that separates from blood on clotting. 3. immune serum; blood serum from an immunized animal used for passive immunization; an antiserum; antitoxin, or antivenin. [EU]

Spasmodic: Of the nature of a spasm. [EU]

Spectrum: A charted band of wavelengths of electromagnetic vibrations obtained by refraction and diffraction. By extension, a measurable range of activity, such as the range of bacteria affected by an antibiotic (antibacterial s.) or the complete range of manifestations of a disease. [EU]

Sporadic: Neither endemic nor epidemic; occurring occasionally in a random or isolated manner. [EU]

Stomach: An organ of digestion situated in the left upper quadrant of the abdomen between the termination of the esophagus and the beginning of the duodenum. [NIH]

Substrate: A substance upon which an enzyme acts. [EU]

Synaptophysin: A 38-kDa integral membrane glycoprotein of the presynaptic vesicles in neuron and neuroendocrine cells. It is expressed by a variety of normal and neoplastic neuroendocrine cells and is therefore used as an immunocytochemical marker for neuroendocrine differentiation in various tumors. In alzheimer disease and other dementing disorders there is an important synapse loss due in part to a decrease of synaptophysin in the presynaptic vesicles. [NIH]

Viral: Pertaining to, caused by, or of the nature of virus. [EU]

Viruses: Minute infectious agents whose genomes are composed of DNA or RNA, but not both. They are characterized by a lack of independent metabolism and the inability to replicate outside living host cells. [NIH]

CHAPTER 5. BOOKS ON APRAXIA

Overview

This chapter provides bibliographic book references relating to apraxia. You have many options to locate books on apraxia. The simplest method is to go to your local bookseller and inquire about titles that they have in stock or can special order for you. Some patients, however, feel uncomfortable approaching their local booksellers and prefer online sources (e.g. **www.amazon.com** and **www.bn.com**). In addition to online booksellers, excellent sources for book titles on apraxia include the Combined Health Information Database and the National Library of Medicine. Once you have found a title that interests you, visit your local public or medical library to see if it is available for loan.

Book Summaries: Federal Agencies

The Combined Health Information Database collects various book abstracts from a variety of healthcare institutions and federal agencies. To access these summaries, go to **http://chid.nih.gov/detail/detail.html**. You will need to use the "Detailed Search" option. To find book summaries, use the drop boxes at the bottom of the search page where "You may refine your search by." Select the dates and language you prefer. For the format option, select "Monograph/Book." Now type "apraxia" (or synonyms) into the "For these words:" box. You will only receive results on books. You should check back periodically with this database which is updated every 3 months. The following is a typical result when searching for books on apraxia:

- **Mentally Impaired Elderly: Strategies and Interventions to Maintain Function**

Source: Binghamton, NY: Haworth Press. 1991. 171 p.

Contact: Available from Haworth Press, Inc. 10 Alice Street, Binghamton, NY 13904-1580. (607) 722-7068 or (800) 342-9678. Price: $29.95. ISBN: 1560241683.

Summary: This book offers guidelines for both professional and personal caregivers of elderly persons with Alzheimer's disease or other mental impairment. Beginning with a theoretical model, interventions are suggested for maintaining the functional level of elderly persons with Alzheimer's disease by focusing on controlling the environment to increase the individual's self care ability. The book describes research on the role of temporal adaptation in self care, the relationship between apraxia and dressing skills, and efforts to enrich the daily lives of institutionalized residents using program enhancement. Other chapters discuss program planning in geriatric psychiatry, approaches to problem behavior, and conflicts in managing elderly parents. References are included at the end of each chapter.

- **Assessment of Aphasia and Related Disorders. 2nd Ed**

Source: Malvern, PA: Lea and Febiger. 1983. [134 p.].

Contact: Available from Lea and Febiger. 200 Chester Field Parkway, Malvern, PA 19355-9725. (610) 251-2230. Price: $47.00 for complete package including the Boston Diagnostic Aphasia Examination Booklet, 16 Test Stimulus Cards, Boston Naming Test, and Boston Naming Test Scoring Booklet. ISBN: 0812109015.

Summary: This book offers some insights into the assessment of aphasia and related disorders that can serve as a bridge to relating test scores to the common aphasic syndromes recognized by neurologists. This book's opening two chapters describes aphasic disorders and the goals and rationale of the assessment procedure. Chapter 3 cites the statistical data available up to 1982. Chapter 4 describes the test procedure, subtest by subtest, and is intended to serve as an instruction manual for the examiner. Chapter 5 describes additional, unstandardized, special language testing procedures, some of which are being investigated and others that are used informally at the Boston University Aphasia Research Center. Chapter 6 describes a supplementary nonverbal battery covering apraxia and the quantitative, visuospatial, and somatognostic problems that, in addition to language, are so often implicated. Chapter 7 describes the major aphasic syndromes, discusses some of the rare pure forms of selective aphasia, and shows how each pattern is reflected in the

Aphasia Test score profile, with the help of selected case summaries. This book includes the Boston Diagnostic Aphasia Examination and 16 stimulus cards.

- **Essentials for Speech-Language Pathologists**

Source: San Diego, CA: Singular Publishing Group. 2001. 468 p.

Contact: Available from Thomson Learning Group. P.O. Box 6904, Florence, KY 41022. (800) 842-3636. Fax (606) 647-5963. Website: www.singpub.com. Price: $49.95 plus shipping and handling. ISBN: 0769300715.

Summary: This textbook is designed to help new professionals with the transition to clinical practice in speech language pathology. The text focuses on professional issues with American Speech-Language-Hearing Association (ASHA) guidelines and practice standards, followed by case law and legislation that dictate professional practice in educational and health care settings, as well as a review of the most common communicative disorders and corresponding assessment and treatment guidelines. Specific disorders covered include aphasia, apraxia, articulation and phonological disorders, attention deficit (hyperactivity) disorder, augmentative and alternative communication (AAC), autism, cleft lip and cleft palate, dementias, dysarthria, dysphagia in adults, fluency disorders, hearing loss, language disorders in children, laryngectomy, multicultural issues in speech language pathology, pediatric feeding problems, reading and spelling disorders, syndromes, traumatic brain injury, and voice disorders. The assessment portion of each chapter reviews basic testing protocol related to the disorder. In some cases, the names of published tests are provided, as well as informal procedures that can be used to assess clients with the disorder. The text concludes with two appendixes: first, standard reading passages used for a variety of assessments; and second a list of resources, including web sites, addresses, and telephone numbers of information organizations; ordering information for AAC devices and laryngectomy equipment; and the names, addresses, and telephone numbers of various companies that offer assessment and therapy materials. A list of references and a subject index conclude the book. The text is recommended reading for students and professionals who are preparing to take the Praxis Examination in Speech Language Pathology. 390 references.

- **Hegde's Pocket Guide to Treatment in Speech-Language Pathology. 2nd edition**

Source: San Diego, CA: Singular Publishing Group. 2001. 576 p.

Contact: Available from Thomson Learning Group. P.O. Box 6904, Florence, KY 41022. (800) 842-3636. Fax (606) 647-5963. Website: www.singpub.com. Price: $49.95 plus shipping and handling. ISBN: 0769301592.

Summary: This pocket guide to treatment procedures in speech language pathology has been designed for clinical practitioners and students in communicative disorders. The guidebook combines a specialized dictionary of terms, clinical resource book, and information typical to textbooks and manuals on treatment. By avoiding theoretical background and controversies, the guide gives the essence of treatment in a step by step format that promotes easy understanding and ready reference just before beginning treatment. Major topics covered are: aphasia (impairment of language comprehension), apraxia of speech (neurogenic speech disorder), articulation and phonological disorders, cerebral palsy, cleft palate, cluttering, dementia, dysarthria (motor speech disorder), dysphagia (swallowing disorders), hearing impairment, language disorders in children, laryngectomy (removal of the larynx), right hemisphere syndrome, stuttering, traumatic brain injury (TBI), and voice disorders. Under each of the main entries for these major disorders, the clinician may then look up subentries or specific types of disorders.

- **Family Guide to Surviving Stroke and Communication Disorders**

Source: Needham Heights, MA: Allyn and Bacon. 1999. 273 p.

Contact: Available from Allyn and Bacon. 160 Gould Street, Needham Heights, MA 02194. (800) 278-3525. Website: www.abacon.com. Price: $20.95. ISBN: 0205285384.

Summary: This book offers families practical information on stroke related communication disorders, particularly aphasia, apraxia, and dysarthrias. Through nontechnical terms, a short story, case studies, questions and answers, and examples, the book engages families, stroke and rehabilitation specialists, and counselors on a journey toward understanding and healing. Twelve chapters cover stroke and the ability to communicate, the loss of language, motor speech disorders, complications, loss of awareness, thinking without language, depression and the stroke survivor, anxiety and the stroke survivor, maintaining relationships, accepting unwanted change, and speech and language rehabilitation. The book includes a glossary of stroke terminology and a subject index. Appendices offer lists of associations and agencies, resources for further reading and research, and a list of aphasia community groups.

- **Neuromotor Speech Disorders: Nature, Assessment, and Management**

Source: Baltimore, MD: Paul H. Brookes Publishing Company. 1998. 339 p.

Contact: Available from Paul H. Brookes Publishing Company. P.O. Box 10624, Baltimore, MD 21285-0624. (800) 638-3775. Fax (410) 337-8539. E-mail: custserv@pbrookes.com. Website: www.brookespublishing.com. Price: $44.95 plus shipping and handling. ISBN: 1557663262.

Summary: This textbook is a compilation of research of interest to speech language pathologists, health care professionals, basic researchers, and students who treat or study pathologies of motor systems affecting speech communication. The 18 chapters contain information about the basic nature of speech motor processes and methods by which they are evaluated; mechanisms of their breakdown in neuropathology; and resultant consequences for the physiological production, acoustic transmission, and understandability of disordered speech. In addition, specific information on the clinical characteristics and management of specific neuromotor speech disorders (e.g., the various dysarthrias, apraxia of speech, spasmodic dysphonia) is presented. One section discusses intelligibility, acceptability, and naturalness (three chapters); another addresses controversial issues in dysphonia (three chapters). Each chapter, written by specialists in the field, includes references, and the text concludes with a subject index.

- **Approaches to the Treatment of Aphasia**

Source: San Diego, CA: Singular Publishing Group, Inc. 1998. 274 p.

Contact: Available from Singular Publishing Group, Inc. 401 West 'A' Street, Suite 325, San Diego, CA 92101-7904. (800) 521-8545 or (619) 238-6777. Fax (800) 774-8398 or (619) 238-6789. E-mail: singpub@singpub.com. Website: www.singpub.com. Price: $49.95 plus shipping and handling. ISBN: 1565938410.

Summary: This book is a collection of reports from clinicians about the clinical management of specific individuals with aphasia. The volume presents readers with an opportunity to eavesdrop on some highly experienced clinicians as they grapple with the very real problems of helping their particular patients. The eight cases were originally presented to other clinicians at a conference in Cody, Wyoming in October 1996. The introductory chapter reviews the historical perspective of using case studies, particularly in the field of aphasia therapy. The other eight chapters each offer one case study, covering issues including a case of aphasia, apraxia of speech, and apraxia of phonation; a strategy for improving oral naming in an individual with a phonological access impairment; a cognitive approach to treatment of an aphasic patient; an experimental treatment of sentence comprehension; treating sentence production in agrammatic aphasia; treatment for letter by letter reading; alexia without agraphia; and treating real life functionality in a couple coping with severe aphasia. A final chapter summarizes the impact on clinical care of a changing health care system. Most chapters conclude with a list of references and the book concludes with a subject index.

- **Desk Reference of Assessment Instruments in Speech and Language**

Source: San Antonio, TX: Communication Skill Builders. 1996. 416 p.

Contact: Available from Communication Skill Builders. Psychological Corporation, Order Service Center, 555 Academic Court, San Antonio, TX 78204-2498. (800) 211-8378; TTY (800) 723-1318; Fax (800) 232-1223. Price: $59.00 plus shipping and handling. ISBN: 0761632255.

Summary: This book, written for clinicians, students, and researchers in speech-language pathology, presents detailed reviews of more than ninety commercially available assessment instruments in speech and language. The authors provide a description of the instrument content, a qualitative evaluation of its effectiveness, and information on publishers and prices. Treatment areas covered include language, articulation, phonology, aphasia, dysarthria, apraxia, head injury, fluency, voice, oral motor skills, auditory processing, early childhood, and special needs. An appendix lists the tests alphabetically by title and includes information about the category, age range, publisher, and price; a second appendix lists publisher's addresses. 113 references. (AA-M).

- **Clinical Aphasiology**

Source: Austin, TX: Pro-Ed. 1996. 293 p.

Contact: Available from Pro-Ed. 8700 Shoal Creek Boulevard, Austin, TX 78757-6897. (800) 897-3202 or (512) 451-3246; Fax (512) 451-8542. Price: $49.00 plus shipping and handling. ISBN: 0890796955.

Summary: This textbook on clinical aphasiology contains original papers first presented at the 1994 Clinical Aphasiology Conference (CAC), held in Traverse City, Michigan. The book is divided into five sections that include consideration of theory-driven clinical research and various scientific, professional, and treatment issues relevant to communication rehabilitation for adults with aphasia and with right-hemisphere dysfunction. The first part, theory in clinical research, presents three manuscripts that highlight the importance of, preparation for, and pitfalls in the inferential chain used in theory building (i.e., theory, experiment, interpretation, theory). The second part, apraxia of speech and phonological output, explores the diagnostically challenging area of motor speech and aphasic output disorders. This section includes a review of acoustic analyses studies in aphasia and apraxia of speech, two acoustic investigations, and two treatment studies. Part Three, diagnostic tests and prognosis for aphasia, delineates the scoring and rationale for The Philadelphia Naming Test, presents the effects of normal aging variables on the Boston Naming Test, compares aphasic performances on two versions of the Revised Token Test, and concludes with longitudinal measures for acute aphasia on the Western Aphasia Battery. Part Four includes information and evidence for a basal temporal language area, question asking strategies, and picture naming variability in adult aphasia. The volume concludes with investigations of right hemisphere processing deficits: proverb interpretation, plausibility judgements, error awareness, and the effects of auditory distractors on comprehension performance. An author index is appended.

- **Communication Problems After a Brain Injury or Stroke**

  Source: Washington, DC: American Association of Retired Persons (AARP). 1994. 12 p.

  Contact: Available from Pritchett and Hull Associates, Inc. 3440 Oakcliff Road, N.E., Suite 110, Atlanta, GA 30340-3079. (800) 241-4925. Price: $3.20 for health professionals; $6.25 retail; plus shipping and handling. ISBN: 0939838443.

  Summary: This booklet is written to help patients and their families and caregivers understand common communication problems that can occur after a brain injury or stroke. Topics include communication and the brain, what happens to the brain during a stroke, the symptoms of communication disorders, using gestures as a basic way to communicate, the role of the speech language pathologist or therapist, aphasia, dysarthria, apraxia, cognitive problems, writing, understanding speech, memory problems, and getting respite. For each of the common communication problems, the authors provide communication strategies to address the disorder. The booklet is illustrated with cartoon-like line drawings depicting a variety of ethnic groups.

- **Communication for the Speechless. 3rd ed**

  Source: Needham Heights, MA: Allyn and Bacon. 1995. 413 p.

  Contact: Available from Allyn and Bacon. 160 Gould Street, Needham, MA 02194-2310. (800) 278-3525 or (617) 455-1200; Fax (515) 284-2607. Price: $50.85 plus shipping and handling. ISBN: 0013184874.

Summary: This textbook provides information about augmentative and alternative communications methods used for children and adults with essentially normal hearing who are without speech. Their speech disorders may have resulted from one or a combination of several conditions, including severe dysarthria, severe verbal apraxia, aphasia, glossectomy, tracheostomy, dysphonia, severe mental retardation, or childhood autism. The first section defines augmentative communication strategies. The author indicates how such strategies have been used with several clinical populations, describes the need for a communication rather than a speech orientation when dealing with persons from these populations, and summarizes the relevant outcome literature. The second section describes and evaluates the various gestural (unaided), gestural-assisted (aided) and neuro-assisted (aided) communication strategies that have been developed. Finally, the author describes an evaluation procedure for selecting the appropriate communication strategy or strategies for each client. The book contains a comprehensive bibliography, a list of sources of materials for teaching the use of augmentative communication strategies, a list of sources of 'components' for communication aids, and a detailed subject index. 2300 references.

- **Motor Speech Disorders: Advances in Assessment and Treatment**

Source: Baltimore, MD: Paul H. Brookes Publishing Company. 1994. 288 p.

Contact: Available from Paul H. Brookes Publishing Company. P.O. Box 10624, Baltimore, MD 21285-0624. (800) 638-3775. Fax (410) 337-8539. E-mail: custserv@pbrookes.com. Website: www.brookespublishing.com. Price: $38.00. ISBN: 1557661375.

Summary: This book is based on selected papers given at the Conference on Motor Speech Disorders held in 1992 at Boulder, Colorado. The book presents seventeen chapters organized into four sections: perspectives on motor speech disorders, clinical characteristics, advances in diagnostic assessment, and approaches to treatment. Specific topics covered include: dysarthria from the viewpoint of individuals with dysarthria; classification of individuals with dysarthria; spasmodic torticollis; Parkinsonian dysarthria; vowel variability in developmental apraxia of speech; the application of instrumental techniques in the assessment of dysarthria; accelerometric difference index for subjects with normal and hypernasal speech; increasing the efficiency of articulatory force testing of adults with traumatic brain injury; tongue function testing in Parkinson's disease; semantic context and speech intelligibility; CPAP therapy for treating hypernasality following closed head injury; accelerating speech in hypokinetic dysarthria; and the effects of syllable characteristics and training on speaking rate in a child with dysarthria secondary to near-drowning. Each chapter includes extensive references and a subject index concludes the text.

- **Developmental Motor Speech Disorders**

  Source: San Diego, CA: Singular Publishing Group, Inc. 1993. 283 p.

  Contact: Available from Singular Publishing Group, Inc. 401 West 'A' Street, Suite 325, San Diego, CA 92101-7904. (800) 521-8545 or (619) 238-6777. Fax (800) 774-8398 or (619) 238-6789. E-mail: singpub@singpub.com. Website: www.singpub.com. Price: $42.50 plus shipping and handling. ISBN: 1879105926.

  Summary: This book presents nine chapters, divided into three sections, on developmental motor speech disorders. Chapter 1 presents a historical perspective focusing on traditional views of developmental dysarthria and apraxia of speech. A neurolinguistic perspective is offered in Chapter 2, in which the underpinnings of an explanatory model are reviewed. This chapter portrays the potential for multiple, interactive problems to exist in the child with a developmental motor speech disorder. A motolinguistic model is presented in Chapter 3. Based on the neurolinguistic principles offered in Chapter 2, this model presents a simplified conceptualization of a continuum of motor and language behaviors. Basic definitions and expected performance profiles are delineated in consideration of this model. Chapters 4 through 7 present performance characteristics of the child with a developmental motor speech disorder. Most of this information is based on work in the area of apraxia of speech, but, when possible, interpretations relevant to dysarthria are offered. Finally, Chapters 8 and 9 offer strategies for clinical assessment of and intervention for the child with a developmental motor speech disorder. A subject index concludes the volume. 6 appendices. 225 references. (AA-M).

- **Introduction to Neurogenic Communication Disorders. 5th ed**

  Source: St. Louis, MO: Mosby-Year Book, Inc. 1992. 506 p.

  Contact: Available from Mosby-Year Book, Inc. 11830 Westline Industrial Drive, P.O. Box 46908, St. Louis, MO 63146. (800) 426-4545 or (314) 872-8370; Fax (800) 535-9935; E-mail: customer.support@mosby.com; http://www.mosby.com. Price: $45.99 plus shipping and handling. ISBN: 0815110146.

  Summary: This textbook provides a basic overview of neurogenic communication disorders, their causes, symptoms, and treatment. These communication disorders include aphasia, brain injuries, dementia, dysarthria, and apraxia. Ten chapters discuss neuroanatomy and neuropathology, neurologic assessment, assessing adults who have neurogenic communication impairments, assessing aphasia and related disorders, the context for treatment of neurogenic communication disorders, treatment of aphasia and related disorders, right hemisphere syndrome, traumatic brain injury (TBI), dementia, and dysarthria. The text concludes with an appendix of standard medical abbreviations, a glossary, bibliography, and index. 566 references.

- **Acquired Aphasia. 2nd Ed**

  Source: Orlando, FL: Academic Press, Inc. 1991. 614 p.

  Contact: Available from Academic Press, Inc. 6277 Sea Harbor Drive, Orlando, FL 32887. (800) 245-8744; Fax (800) 874-6418. Price: $64.95 plus shipping and handling. ISBN: 0126193215.

  Summary: This textbook brings together the writing of some well known workers in the field of aphasia. Sixteen chapters cover historical perspectives, signs of aphasia, neuroanatomical correlates of the aphasias, assessment, phonological aspects of aphasia, lexical deficits, sentence processing, explanations for the concept of apraxia of speech, aphasia-related disorders, intelligence and aphasia, artistry and aphasia, language in aging and dementia, acquired aphasia in children, aphasia after head injury, the psychological and social sequelae of aphasia, and recovery and rehabilitation considerations. Each chapter includes extensive references, and the text concludes with a subject index. The editor notes that the scope of this volume does not permit a review of the techniques and practice of aphasia therapy, but instead outlines broad principles.

Book Summaries: Online Booksellers

Commercial Internet-based booksellers, such as Amazon.com and Barnes & Noble.com, offer summaries which have been supplied by each title's publisher. Some summaries also include customer reviews. Your local bookseller may have access to in-house and commercial databases that index all published books (e.g. Books in Print®).

The National Library of Medicine Book Index

The National Library of Medicine at the National Institutes of Health has a massive database of books published on healthcare and biomedicine. Go to the following Internet site, **http://locatorplus.gov/**, and then select "Search LOCATORplus." Once you are in the search area, simply type "apraxia" (or synonyms) into the search box, and select "books only." From there, results can be sorted by publication date, author, or relevance. The following was recently catalogued by the National Library of Medicine:[20]

- **Acquired apraxia of speech in aphasic adults: theoretical and clinical issues.** Author: edited by Paula Square-Storer; Year: 1989; London; New York: Taylor ; Francis, 1989; ISBN: 0850664497
  http://www.amazon.com/exec/obidos/ASIN/0850664497/icongroupin
  terna

- **Agnosia and apraxia: selected papers of Liepmann, Lange, and Pötzl.** Author: edited by Jason W. Brown; translations by George Dean ... [et al.]; Year: 1988; Hillsdale, N.J.: L. Erlbaum Associates, 1988; ISBN: 080580286X
  http://www.amazon.com/exec/obidos/ASIN/080580286X/icongroupi
  nterna

- **Agnosia, apraxia, aphasia; their value in cerebral localization, by J. M. Nielsen ...** Author: Nielsen, Johannes Maagaard, 1890-; Year: 1946; New York, London, P. B. Hoeber, inc. [1946]

- **Aphasia, apraxia and agnosia; clinical and theoretical aspects.** Author: Brown, Jason W; Year: 1972; Springfield, Ill., Thomas [c1972]; ISBN: 0398022119
  http://www.amazon.com/exec/obidos/ASIN/0398022119/icongroupin
  terna

- **Apraxia: the neuropsychology of action.** Author: edited by Leslie J. Gonzalez Rothi and Kenneth M. Heilman; Year: 1997; Hove, East Sussex, UK: Psychology Press, c1997; ISBN: 0863777430
  http://www.amazon.com/exec/obidos/ASIN/0863777430/icongroupin
  terna

---

[20] In addition to LOCATORPlus, in collaboration with authors and publishers, the National Center for Biotechnology Information (NCBI) is adapting biomedical books for the Web. The books may be accessed in two ways: (1) by searching directly using any search term or phrase (in the same way as the bibliographic database PubMed), or (2) by following the links to PubMed abstracts. Each PubMed abstract has a "Books" button that displays a facsimile of the abstract in which some phrases are hypertext links. These phrases are also found in the books available at NCBI. Click on hyperlinked results in the list of books in which the phrase is found. Currently, the majority of the links are between the books and PubMed. In the future, more links will be created between the books and other types of information, such as gene and protein sequences and macromolecular structures. See **http://www.ncbi.nlm.nih.gov/entrez/query.fcgi?db=Books.**

- **Apraxia in stroke patients: assessment and treatment.** Author: Carolina Maria van Heugten; Year: 1998; [Utrecht]: NIVEL, [1998?]; ISBN: 9069053845

- **Apraxia of speech: physiology, acoustics, linguistics, management.** Author: edited by John C. Rosenbek, Malcolm R. McNeil, Arnold E. Aronson; Year: 1984; San Diego, Calif.: College-Hill Press, c1984; ISBN: 0933014082 (pbk.)
  http://www.amazon.com/exec/obidos/ASIN/0933014082/icongroupin terna

- **Apraxia of speech in adults: the disorder and its management.** Author: Robert T. Wertz, Leonard L. LaPointe, John C. Rosenbek; Year: 1984; Orlando, Fla.: Grune ; Stratton, c1984; ISBN: 0808916122
  http://www.amazon.com/exec/obidos/ASIN/0808916122/icongroupin terna

- **Apraxia. [Translated by Lottie B. Applewhite.** Author: Liepmann, Heinz, 1905-; Year: 1969; San Francisco, 1969]

- **Apraxia; bibliography. 146 references: 1966-1973; period of search: 1968-May 1973.** Author: Information Center for Hearing, Speech, and Disorders of Human Communication; Year: 1973; Baltimore, 1973

- **Assessment and treatment of developmental apraxia.** Author: Dorothy M. Aram; Year: 1984; New York: Thieme-Stratton, c1984

- **Developmental apraxia of speech: theory and clinical practice.** Author: Penelope K. Hall, Linda S. Jordan, Donald A. Robin; Year: 1993; Austin, Tex.: Pro-Ed, c1993; ISBN: 0890795827
  http://www.amazon.com/exec/obidos/ASIN/0890795827/icongroupin terna

- **Dysarthria and apraxia of speech: perspectives on management.** Author: edited by Christopher A. Moore, Kathryn M. Yorkston, and David R. Beukelman; Year: 1991; Baltimore: Brookes Pub. Co., c1991; ISBN: 1557660697
  http://www.amazon.com/exec/obidos/ASIN/1557660697/icongroupin terna

- **Dysarthria and apraxia.** Author: edited by William H. Perkins; Year: 1983; New York: Thieme-Stratton, 1983; ISBN: 0865770867
  http://www.amazon.com/exec/obidos/ASIN/0865770867/icongroupin terna

- **Neuropsychological studies of apraxia and related disorders.** Author: edited by Eric A. Roy; Year: 1985; Amsterdam; New York: North-Holland; New York, N.Y., U.S.A.: Sole distributors for the U.S.A. and Canada, Elsevier Science Pub. Co., 1985; ISBN: 0444876693 (U.S.)

http://www.amazon.com/exec/obidos/ASIN/0444876693/icongroupin
terna

- **Speech disorders: aphasia, apraxia, and agnosia.**   Author: Brain, W. Russell Brain (Walter Russell Brain), Baron, 1895-1966; Year: 1961; London, Butterworth, 1961

- **Take time to talk: a resource for apraxia therapy, esophageal speech training, aphasia therapy, and articulation therapy.**   Author: Patricia F. White; Year: 1996; Boston: Butterworth-Heinemann, c1996; ISBN: 0750697830 (pbk.: alk. paper)

  http://www.amazon.com/exec/obidos/ASIN/0750697830/icongroupin
  terna

- **Treating disordered speech motor control: for clinicians by clinicians.** Author: edited by Deanie Vogel and Michael P. Cannito; Year: 2001; Austin, Tex.: Pro-Ed, c2001; ISBN: 0890798699

  http://www.amazon.com/exec/obidos/ASIN/0890798699/icongroupin
  terna

Chapters on Apraxia

Frequently, apraxia will be discussed within a book, perhaps within a specific chapter. In order to find chapters that are specifically dealing with apraxia, an excellent source of abstracts is the Combined Health Information Database. You will need to limit your search to book chapters and apraxia using the "Detailed Search" option. Go directly to the following hyperlink: **http://chid.nih.gov/detail/detail.html**. To find book chapters, use the drop boxes at the bottom of the search page where "You may refine your search by." Select the dates and language you prefer, and the format option "Book Chapter." By making these selections and typing in "apraxia" (or synonyms) into the "For these words:" box, you will only receive results on chapters in books. The following is a typical result when searching for book chapters on apraxia:

- **Apraxia**

  Source: in Vinson, B.P. Essentials for Speech-Language Pathologists. San Diego, CA: Singular Publishing Group. 2001. p. 99-113.

  Contact: Available from Thomson Learning Group. P.O. Box 6904, Florence, KY 41022. (800) 842-3636. Fax (606) 647-5963. Website: www.singpub.com. Price: $49.95 plus shipping and handling. ISBN: 0769300715.

Summary: Apraxia is a neurogenic (nervous system based) speech disorder resulting from sensorimotor impairment of the ability to program and execute the muscles used to create speech. Acquired apraxia of speech may occur as the result of a stroke, traumatic brain injury, or tumor. This chapter on apraxia is from a textbook that is designed to help new professionals with the transition to clinical practice in speech language pathology. The author notes that in apraxia, the most frequent misarticulations are omissions and substitutions. Also, the number of misarticulations typically increases when the complexity of the speech task increases. Developmental apraxia of speech (DAOS) typically occurs at a time when children are acquiring language and includes inability to perform or difficulty performing the purposeful voluntary movements for speech. The author discusses assessment tools and strategies, followed by a section on treatment options. The specific speech tasks that need to be covered are listed, from easy to more difficult tasks. The chapter concludes with two appendixes: checklists for limb, oral, and verbal apraxia; and suggested words for imitation when assessing speech apraxia. 5 tables.

- **Phonological Analysis of Apraxia of Speech in Broca's Aphasia**

Source: in Cannito, M.P.; Yorkston, K.M.; Beukelman, D.R., eds. Neuromotor Speech Disorders: Nature, Assessment, and Management. Baltimore, MD: Paul H. Brookes Publishing Company. 1998. p. 309-321.

Contact: Available from Paul H. Brookes Publishing Company. P.O. Box 10624, Baltimore, MD 21285-0624. (800) 638-3775. Fax (410) 337-8539. E-mail: custserv@pbrookes.com. Website: www.brookespublishing.com. Price: $44.95 plus shipping and handling. ISBN: 1557663262.

Summary: This chapter is from a textbook offering a compilation of research of interest to speech language pathologists, health care professionals, basic researchers, and students who treat or study pathologies of motor systems affecting speech communication. This chapter discusses the phonological analysis of apraxia of speech in Broca's aphasia. The authors present a study in which they describe the speech of 10 subjects with Broca's aphasia and apraxia of speech. The authors assume a phonological analytic vantage point to address the issue of potential linguistic explanations for observed speech output characteristics of apraxia in Broca's aphasia. Subjects had clinical characteristics of effortful, groping articulation; speech dysprosody; variable articulation errors; and other symptomatology congruent with the diagnosis of apraxia of speech. The results failed to reveal evidence that subjects with Broca's aphasia exhibit impairment in phonological ability. Error rates were low with limited use of phonological processes.

The results support a motor programming interpretation of apraxia of speech as manifested in Broca's aphasia, as opposed to an underlying deficit at the phonological level of language processing. 4 figures. 2 tables. 23 references.

- **Phonemic Retrieval in Apraxia of Speech Revisited: Additional Evidence for More Than One Type of Impairment**

Source: in Cannito, M.P.; Yorkston, K.M.; Beukelman, D.R., eds. Neuromotor Speech Disorders: Nature, Assessment, and Management. Baltimore, MD: Paul H. Brookes Publishing Company. 1998. p. 323-332.

Contact: Available from Paul H. Brookes Publishing Company. P.O. Box 10624, Baltimore, MD 21285-0624. (800) 638-3775. Fax (410) 337-8539. E-mail: custserv@pbrookes.com. Website: www.brookespublishing.com. Price: $44.95 plus shipping and handling. ISBN: 1557663262.

Summary: This chapter is from a textbook offering a compilation of research of interest to speech language pathologists, health care professionals, basic researchers, and students who treat or study pathologies of motor systems affecting speech communication. This chapter considers phonemic retrieval in apraxia of speech. The authors note that word retrieval is an interactive process constrained by the nature of a task. Information retained for short periods is dependent on a multicomponent short term memory system (working memory). This chapter reports on a study that compared the similarities and differences between two adult subjects with apraxia of speech (AOS). The successful attempts at deferred repetition for Subject 1 were compared with those of Subject 2 as a means of providing additional evidence for two different subtypes of AOS. The study also highlights the function and specifics of the central executive control (CEC) system, particularly emphasizing the role of the supervisory attentional system on speech production. 1 figure. 4 tables. 19 references.

- **Apraxia of Speech: Another Form of Praxis Disruption**

Source: in Rothi, L.J. and Heilman, K.M., eds. Apraxia: The Neuropsychology of Action. East Sussex, United Kingdom: Psychology Press. 1997. p. 173-206.

Contact: Available from Taylor and Francis. Rankine Road, Basingstoke, Hampshire, RG248PR, England. +44(0)1256 813000. Fax +44(0)1256 479438. Price: $39.95. ISBN: 0863777430.

Summary: This chapter on apraxia of speech is from a neuropsychology textbook on apraxia. The authors of this chapter focus only on the manner in which aspects of speech production processes are altered as a result of damage to the left hemisphere of the brain. The discussion provides evidence indicating that language and sensorimotor speech processes may be independently disrupted as a result of left hemisphere brain damage. The authors then provide a general discussion of the neurophysiology of motor control. Preliminary evidence is provided which demonstrates that several variations of motor speech implementation difficulties may arise from left hemisphere damage. Hypotheses regarding the nature and variations of motor speech disorders subsequent to left-hemisphere brain damage are also discussed. The final sections of the chapter review the similarities between speech, buccofacial, and limb apraxia with regard to lesion sites associated with the disorders and resulting behaviors as measured both behaviorally and physiologically. The chapter concludes with a brief review of motor speech treatments for apraxia of speech. 1 table. 185 references.

- **Dysarthria-Apraxia**

Source: in Harris, L.G.; Shelton, I.S. Desk Reference of Assessments in Speech-Language. Tucson, AZ: Communication Skill Builders. 1993. p. 165-174.

Contact: Available from Communication Skill Builders. 3830 East Bellvue, P.O. Box 42050, Tucson, AZ 85733. Voice (602) 323-7500; Fax (606) 325-0306. Price: $59.00 plus shipping and handling. ISBN: 0884506320.

Summary: This chapter, from a reference book on current speech and language testing instruments, presents detailed reviews of assessments in the area of dysarthria/apraxia. Four instruments are reviewed, including the Apraxia Battery for Adults; the Assessment of Intelligibility of Dysarthric Speakers; Frenchay Dysarthria Assessment; and the Screening Test for Developmental Apraxia of Speech. For each entry, the authors provide a detailed description of the instrument content, an evaluation of its effectiveness, and current information on publishers and prices. The chapter also includes details regarding standardization data (reliability and validity), administrative considerations, and scoring.

- **Social Apraxia of Epilepsy**

Source: in Psychological Disturbances in Epilepsy. Sackellares, J.C.; Berent, S.; eds. Boston, MA, Butterworth-Heinemann, pp. 159-170, 1996.

Contact: Butterworth-Heinemann, 313 Washington Street, Newton, MA 02158-1626.

Summary: The Social Apraxia of Epilepsy, a chapter in Psychological Disturbances in Epilepsy, proposes a model of social apraxia to explain the interpersonal difficulties of people with epilepsy. The first part examines the definition of personality, symptoms of personality disorder, and the concept of epileptic personality, and provides a historical perspective on theories of epilepsy and personality. The second part uses the metaphor of social apraxia to explain the epileptic personality, describing it as an expression of attentional impairments. Social apraxia is associated with perceptual disturbances that result in misinterpretation of social cues, impaired affective modulation, difficulty prioritizing goals and drives, impaired capacity to construct and modify maps of the social environment, and clumsy execution and communication of intentions in a social arena. The model enables clinicians to examine the problems experienced by many people with epilepsy without the moral characterization which has shaped the debate over epileptic personality. It also can guide efforts to help patients with epileptic personalities improve their impaired adaptation to the demands of social life. These patients may benefit from such interventions as communication skills training, rehearsal of adaptive responses, anger management training, assertiveness training, role playing with peers, and pharmacologic treatment. The chapter includes a case study illustrating the effects of epilepsy on personality and the benefits of intervention.

General Home References

In addition to references for apraxia, you may want a general home medical guide that spans all aspects of home healthcare. The following list is a recent sample of such guides (sorted alphabetically by title; hyperlinks provide rankings, information, and reviews at Amazon.com):

- **Adams & Victor's Principles Of Neurology** by Maurice Victor, et al; Hardcover - 1692 pages; 7th edition (December 19, 2000), McGraw-Hill Professional Publishing; ISBN: 0070674973; http://www.amazon.com/exec/obidos/ASIN/0070674973/icongroupinterna

- **Clinical Neuroanatomy Made Ridiculously Simple (MedMaster Series, 2000 Edition)** by Stephen Goldberg; Paperback: 97 pages; 2nd edition (February 15, 2000), Medmaster; ISBN: 0940780461; http://www.amazon.com/exec/obidos/ASIN/0940780461/icongroupinterna

- **It's Not a Tumor!: The Patient's Guide to Common Neurological Problems** by Robert Wiedemeyer; Paperback: (January 1996), Boxweed Pub; ISBN: 0964740796; http://www.amazon.com/exec/obidos/ASIN/0964740796/icongroupinterna

- **Neurology for the Non-Neurologist** by William J. Weiner (Editor), Christopher G. Goetz (Editor); Paperback (May 1999), Lippincott, Williams & Wilkins Publishers; ISBN: 0781717078; http://www.amazon.com/exec/obidos/ASIN/0781717078/icongroupinterna

Vocabulary Builder

Anxiety: The unpleasant emotional state consisting of psychophysiological responses to anticipation of unreal or imagined danger, ostensibly resulting from unrecognized intrapsychic conflict. Physiological concomitants include increased heart rate, altered respiration rate, sweating, trembling, weakness, and fatigue; psychological concomitants include feelings of impending danger, powerlessness, apprehension, and tension. [EU]

Cues: Signals for an action; that specific portion of a perceptual field or pattern of stimuli to which a subject has learned to respond. [NIH]

Gestures: Movement of a part of the body for the purpose of communication. [NIH]

Localization: 1. the determination of the site or place of any process or lesion. 2. restriction to a circumscribed or limited area. 3. prelocalization. [EU]

Neuroanatomy: Study of the anatomy of the nervous system as a specialty or discipline. [NIH]

Symptomatology: 1. that branch of medicine with treats of symptoms; the systematic discussion of symptoms. 2. the combined symptoms of a disease. [EU]

Torticollis: Wryneck; a contracted state of the cervical muscles, producing twisting of the neck and an unnatural position of the head. [EU]

Tracheostomy: Surgical formation of an opening into the trachea through the neck, or the opening so created. [NIH]

Translations: Products resulting from the conversion of one language to another. [NIH]

CHAPTER 6. MULTIMEDIA ON APRAXIA

Overview

Information on apraxia can come in a variety of formats. Among multimedia sources, video productions, slides, audiotapes, and computer databases are often available. In this chapter, we show you how to keep current on multimedia sources of information on apraxia. We start with sources that have been summarized by federal agencies, and then show you how to find bibliographic information catalogued by the National Library of Medicine. If you see an interesting item, visit your local medical library to check on the availability of the title.

Video Recordings

Most diseases do not have a video dedicated to them. If they do, they are often rather technical in nature. An excellent source of multimedia information on apraxia is the Combined Health Information Database. You will need to limit your search to "video recording" and "apraxia" using the "Detailed Search" option. Go directly to the following hyperlink: **http://chid.nih.gov/detail/detail.html**. To find video productions, use the drop boxes at the bottom of the search page where "You may refine your search by." Select the dates and language you prefer, and the format option "Videorecording (videotape, videocassette, etc.)." By making these selections and typing "apraxia" (or synonyms) into the "For these words:" box, you will only receive results on video productions. The following is a typical result when searching for video recordings on apraxia:

- **Confusion**

    Source: Baltimore, MD: University of Maryland Video Press. 1993.

Contact: Availabile from the University of Maryland Video Press. 100 North Greene Street, Suite 300, Baltimore, MD 21201. (800) 328-7450 or (410) 706-5497 or FAX (410) 706-5497. Price: $150.00. Also available as part of AZAV07855, a 7-video set (price for set: $950.00).

Summary: This video, which features narration by Dr. Peter Rabins, coauthor of the '36-Hour Day,' and footage of actual patients, explores the underlying causes of confusion in Alzheimer's disease (AD) patients and discusses strategies for managing this problem. Confusion is common among nursing home residents, especially those suffering from AD. Four categories of AD symptoms contribute to confusion: amnesia (inability to learn new things), aphasia (inability to communicate effectively), apraxia (inability to do things), and agnosia (impaired perceptual ability). Medications, illness, environmental changes, and depression may add to confusion. When developing care plans for confused patients, caregivers should first identify the cause of confusion, then explore different management strategies. Effective strategies include reorientation, simplifying environment and activities, using gestures in addition to verbal cues, and eliminating sources of anxiety or frustration.

- **Identification of Motor Speech Disorders**

Source: Rockville, MD: American Speech-Hearing-Language Association (ASHA). 1997. (videocassette and study guide).

Contact: Available from American Speech-Language-Hearing Association (ASHA). Product Sales, 10801 Rockville Pike, Rockville, MD 20852. (888) 498-6699. TTY (301) 897-0157. Website: www.asha.org. Price: $120.00 for ASHA members; $130.00 for nonmembers; plus shipping and handling. ISBN: 1580410103.

Summary: This video conference (designed for self study) offers an opportunity for clinicians to sharpen their ability to differentially diagnose motor speech disorders (the dysarthria and apraxia of speech). This includes presentation and subsequent discussion of numerous audio and videotape samples of people with a wide variety of motor speech disorders (MSD). Clinicians are asked to identify salient and confirmatory features of the speech disorders and to draw conclusions about the type of MSD and its implications for lesion localization. Clinicians are taught to express their diagnostic conclusions in a manner that can assist in the localization and diagnosis of neurologic disease. Topics covered in the manual and accompanying videotape include: the importance of this differential diagnosis of MSDs, basic categorization and definitions of the dysarthrias, assessment principles and procedures, flaccid dysarthria, spastic dysarthria, ataxic dysarthria, hypokinetic dysarthria, hyperkinetic dysarthria, unilateral upper motor neuron dysarthria, mixed dysarthria, and apraxia of speech. The self study unit includes a pretraining assessment and a posttraining assessment. In addition, the manual offers reprinted articles that are relevant to the diagnosis of MSDs. 11 appendices. 16 references.

- **Cerebral Localization of Production Deficits in Aphasia**

  Source: Tucson, AZ: National Center for Neurogenic Communication Disorders, University of Arizona. March 31, 1993. (videocassette and handout).

  Contact: Available from National Center for Neurogenic Communication Disorders. University of Arizona, P.O. Box 210071, Tucson, AZ 85721-0071. (602) 621-1819 or (602) 621-1787. Price: $25.00 plus shipping and handling.

  Summary: This videotape program discusses a new method of evaluating the relationship between lesion site and specific speech and language disorders. Three new findings with regard to the neuroanatomic correlates of non-fluent production problems in aphasia are introduced. First, the consistent relationship between apraxia of speech and a particular area of the insula is presented. Next, the involvement of the arcuate fasciculus is discussed in conjunction with the severe production problems characterized by recurring utterances. Finally, the possibility that the angular gyrus might be involved in agrammatic behavior is explored. 26 references. (AA).

Bibliography: Multimedia on Apraxia

The National Library of Medicine is a rich source of information on healthcare-related multimedia productions including slides, computer software, and databases. To access the multimedia database, go to the following Web site: **http://locatorplus.gov/**. Select "Search LOCATORplus." Once in the search area, simply type in apraxia (or synonyms). Then, in the option box provided below the search box, select "Audiovisuals and Computer Files." From there, you can choose to sort results by publication date, author, or relevance. The following multimedia has been indexed on apraxia. For more information, follow the hyperlink indicated:

- **Oculomotor apraxia (acquired).** Source: United States Army; Year: 1966; Format: Motion picture; [Washington]: The Army; [Jersey City, N. J.: for loan by Conrad Berens International Eye Film Library; Atlanta: for loan by National Medical Audiovisual Center], 1966

- **Real world effects of limb apraxia.** Source: produced by the National Center for Neurogenic Communication Disorders of the University of Arizona [with] Veterans Health Administration, Office of Academic Affairs [and] Long Beach Regional Medical E; Year: 1994; Format: Videorecording; [Tucson, Ariz.]: Arizona Board of Regents, c1994
- **Stroke : focus on apraxia and aphasia.** Source: an AREN production; [produced at the facilities of WQED/Pittsburgh by QED Enterprises]; Year: 1986; Format: Videorecording; [Pittsburgh, Pa.]: AREN, c1986
- **Verbal impairment associated with brain damage.** Source: Institute of Physical Medicine and Rehabilitation, New York University Medical Center; produced by Public Health Service Audiovisual Facility; Year: 1966; Format: Motion picture; Atlanta: National Medical Audiovisual Center; [Washington: for sale by National Audiovisual Center, 1966]

Vocabulary Builder

Amnesia: Lack or loss of memory; inability to remember past experiences. [EU]

Flaccid: Weak, lax and soft. [EU]

Spastic: 1. of the nature of or characterized by spasms. 2. hypertonic, so that the muscles are stiff and the movements awkward. 3. a person exhibiting spasticity, such as occurs in spastic paralysis or in cerebral palsy. [EU]

CHAPTER 7. PERIODICALS AND NEWS ON APRAXIA

Overview

Keeping up on the news relating to apraxia can be challenging. Subscribing to targeted periodicals can be an effective way to stay abreast of recent developments on apraxia. Periodicals include newsletters, magazines, and academic journals.

In this chapter, we suggest a number of news sources and present various periodicals that cover apraxia beyond and including those which are published by patient associations mentioned earlier. We will first focus on news services, and then on periodicals. News services, press releases, and newsletters generally use more accessible language, so if you do chose to subscribe to one of the more technical periodicals, make sure that it uses language you can easily follow.

News Services & Press Releases

Well before articles show up in newsletters or the popular press, they may appear in the form of a press release or a public relations announcement. One of the simplest ways of tracking press releases on apraxia is to search the news wires. News wires are used by professional journalists, and have existed since the invention of the telegraph. Today, there are several major "wires" that are used by companies, universities, and other organizations to announce new medical breakthroughs. In the following sample of sources, we will briefly describe how to access each service. These services only post recent news intended for public viewing.

PR Newswire

Perhaps the broadest of the wires is PR Newswire Association, Inc. To access this archive, simply go to **http://www.prnewswire.com**. Below the search box, select the option "The last 30 days." In the search box, type "apraxia" or synonyms. The search results are shown by order of relevance. When reading these press releases, do not forget that the sponsor of the release may be a company or organization that is trying to sell a particular product or therapy. Their views, therefore, may be biased.

Reuters

The Reuters' Medical News database can be very useful in exploring news archives relating to apraxia. While some of the listed articles are free to view, others can be purchased for a nominal fee. To access this archive, go to **http://www.reutershealth.com/frame2/arch.html** and search by "apraxia" (or synonyms).

The NIH

Within MEDLINEplus, the NIH has made an agreement with the New York Times Syndicate, the AP News Service, and Reuters to deliver news that can be browsed by the public. Search news releases at **http://www.nlm.nih.gov/medlineplus/alphanews_a.html**. MEDLINEplus allows you to browse across an alphabetical index. Or you can search by date at **http://www.nlm.nih.gov/medlineplus/newsbydate.html**. Often, news items are indexed by MEDLINEplus within their search engine.

Business Wire

Business Wire is similar to PR Newswire. To access this archive, simply go to **http://www.businesswire.com**. You can scan the news by industry category or company name.

Internet Wire

Internet Wire is more focused on technology than the other wires. To access this site, go to **http://www.internetwire.com** and use the "Search Archive" option. Type in "apraxia" (or synonyms). As this service is oriented to technology, you may wish to search for press releases covering diagnostic procedures or tests that you may have read about.

Search Engines

Free-to-view news can also be found in the news section of your favorite search engines (see the health news page at Yahoo: **http://dir.yahoo.com/Health/News_and_Media/,** or use this Web site's general news search page **http://news.yahoo.com/.** Type in "apraxia" (or synonyms). If you know the name of a company that is relevant to apraxia, you can go to any stock trading Web site (such as **www.etrade.com**) and search for the company name there. News items across various news sources are reported on indicated hyperlinks.

BBC

Covering news from a more European perspective, the British Broadcasting Corporation (BBC) allows the public free access to their news archive located at **http://www.bbc.co.uk/**. Search by "apraxia" (or synonyms).

Newsletter Articles

If you choose not to subscribe to a newsletter, you can nevertheless find references to newsletter articles. We recommend that you use the Combined Health Information Database, while limiting your search criteria to "newsletter articles." Again, you will need to use the "Detailed Search" option. Go directly to the following hyperlink: **http://chid.nih.gov/detail/detail.html**. Go to the bottom of the search page where "You may refine your search by." Select the dates and language that you prefer. For the format option, select "Newsletter Article."

By making these selections, and typing in "apraxia" (or synonyms) into the "For these words:" box, you will only receive results on newsletter articles. You should check back periodically with this database as it is updated every 3 months. The following is a typical result when searching for newsletter articles on apraxia:

- **Speech After Stroke: Rehabilitation Enhances Recovery and Lifestyle**

  Source: Mayo Clinic Health Letter. 14(8): 1-3. August 1996.

Contact: Available from Mayo Foundation for Medical Education and Research. 200 First Street, S.W., Rochester, MN 55905. (800) 633-4567. Price: $3.00 for single copy of newsletter plus shipping and handling.

Summary: This newsletter article describes advances in post-stroke speech and language rehabilitation. Topics include how stroke damages brain cells; the three main stroke-related communication disorders, aphasia, dysarthria, and apraxia; how speech rehabilitation can enhance quality of life for people who have had a stroke; diagnosing speech and language problems; the components of a speech rehabilitation program, including exercise and practice, and the use of picture cards, picture boards, workbooks, and computers; and the psychosocial impact of recovering from a stroke. One sidebar outlines the role of family and friends in the recovery process.

Academic Periodicals covering Apraxia

Academic periodicals can be a highly technical yet valuable source of information on apraxia. We have compiled the following list of periodicals known to publish articles relating to apraxia and which are currently indexed within the National Library of Medicine's PubMed database (follow hyperlinks to view more information, summaries, etc., for each). In addition to these sources, to keep current on articles written on apraxia published by any of the periodicals listed below, you can simply follow the hyperlink indicated or go to the following Web site: **www.ncbi.nlm.nih.gov/pubmed**. Type the periodical's name into the search box to find the latest studies published.

If you want complete details about the historical contents of a periodical, you can also visit **http://www.ncbi.nlm.nih.gov/entrez/jrbrowser.cgi**. Here, type in the name of the journal or its abbreviation, and you will receive an index of published articles. At **http://locatorplus.gov/** you can retrieve more indexing information on medical periodicals (e.g. the name of the publisher). Select the button "Search LOCATORplus." Then type in the name of the journal and select the advanced search option "Journal Title Search." The following is a sample of periodicals which publish articles on apraxia:

- **Brain and Cognition. (Brain Cogn)**
  http://www.ncbi.nlm.nih.gov/entrez/jrbrowser.cgi?field=0&regexp=Brain+and+Cognition&dispmax=20&dispstart=0

- **Brain and Language. (Brain Lang)**
  http://www.ncbi.nlm.nih.gov/entrez/jrbrowser.cgi?field=0&regexp=Brain+and+Language&dispmax=20&dispstart=0

- **European Neurology. (Eur Neurol)**
  http://www.ncbi.nlm.nih.gov/entrez/jrbrowser.cgi?field=0&regexp=European+Neurology&dispmax=20&dispstart=0

- **Journal of Speech, Language, and Hearing Research : Jslhr. (J Speech Lang Hear Res)**
  http://www.ncbi.nlm.nih.gov/entrez/jrbrowser.cgi?field=0&regexp=Journal+of+Speech,+Language,+and+Hearing+Research+:+Jslhr&dispmax=20&dispstart=0

CHAPTER 8. PHYSICIAN GUIDELINES AND DATABASES

Overview

Doctors and medical researchers rely on a number of information sources to help patients with their conditions. Many will subscribe to journals or newsletters published by their professional associations or refer to specialized textbooks or clinical guides published for the medical profession. In this chapter, we focus on databases and Internet-based guidelines created or written for this professional audience.

NIH Guidelines

For the more common diseases, The National Institutes of Health publish guidelines that are frequently consulted by physicians. Publications are typically written by one or more of the various NIH Institutes. For physician guidelines, commonly referred to as "clinical" or "professional" guidelines, you can visit the following Institutes:

- Office of the Director (OD); guidelines consolidated across agencies available at **http://www.nih.gov/health/consumer/conkey.htm**

- National Institute of General Medical Sciences (NIGMS); fact sheets available at **http://www.nigms.nih.gov/news/facts/**

- National Library of Medicine (NLM); extensive encyclopedia (A.D.A.M., Inc.) with guidelines:
  http://www.nlm.nih.gov/medlineplus/healthtopics.html

- National Institute of Neurological Disorders and Stroke (NINDS); neurological disorder information pages available at
  http://www.ninds.nih.gov/health_and_medical/disorder_index.htm

NIH Databases

In addition to the various Institutes of Health that publish professional guidelines, the NIH has designed a number of databases for professionals.[21] Physician-oriented resources provide a wide variety of information related to the biomedical and health sciences, both past and present. The format of these resources varies. Searchable databases, bibliographic citations, full text articles (when available), archival collections, and images are all available. The following are referenced by the National Library of Medicine:[22]

- **Bioethics:** Access to published literature on the ethical, legal and public policy issues surrounding healthcare and biomedical research. This information is provided in conjunction with the Kennedy Institute of Ethics located at Georgetown University, Washington, D.C.: **http://www.nlm.nih.gov/databases/databases_bioethics.html**

- **HIV/AIDS Resources:** Describes various links and databases dedicated to HIV/AIDS research: **http://www.nlm.nih.gov/pubs/factsheets/aidsinfs.html**

- **NLM Online Exhibitions:** Describes "Exhibitions in the History of Medicine": **http://www.nlm.nih.gov/exhibition/exhibition.html**. Additional resources for historical scholarship in medicine: **http://www.nlm.nih.gov/hmd/hmd.html**

- **Biotechnology Information:** Access to public databases. The National Center for Biotechnology Information conducts research in computational biology, develops software tools for analyzing genome data, and disseminates biomedical information for the better understanding of molecular processes affecting human health and disease: **http://www.ncbi.nlm.nih.gov/**

- **Population Information:** The National Library of Medicine provides access to worldwide coverage of population, family planning, and related health issues, including family planning technology and programs, fertility, and population law and policy: **http://www.nlm.nih.gov/databases/databases_population.html**

- **Cancer Information:** Access to caner-oriented databases: **http://www.nlm.nih.gov/databases/databases_cancer.html**

---

[21] Remember, for the general public, the National Library of Medicine recommends the databases referenced in MEDLINE*plus* (**http://medlineplus.gov/** or **http://www.nlm.nih.gov/medlineplus/databases.html**).
[22] See **http://www.nlm.nih.gov/databases/databases.html**.

- **Profiles in Science:** Offering the archival collections of prominent twentieth-century biomedical scientists to the public through modern digital technology: **http://www.profiles.nlm.nih.gov/**

- **Chemical Information:** Provides links to various chemical databases and references: **http://sis.nlm.nih.gov/Chem/ChemMain.html**

- **Clinical Alerts:** Reports the release of findings from the NIH-funded clinical trials where such release could significantly affect morbidity and mortality: **http://www.nlm.nih.gov/databases/alerts/clinical_alerts.html**

- **Space Life Sciences:** Provides links and information to space-based research (including NASA):
  http://www.nlm.nih.gov/databases/databases_space.html

- **MEDLINE:** Bibliographic database covering the fields of medicine, nursing, dentistry, veterinary medicine, the healthcare system, and the pre-clinical sciences:
  http://www.nlm.nih.gov/databases/databases_medline.html

- **Toxicology and Environmental Health Information (TOXNET):** Databases covering toxicology and environmental health:
  http://sis.nlm.nih.gov/Tox/ToxMain.html

- **Visible Human Interface:** Anatomically detailed, three-dimensional representations of normal male and female human bodies:
  http://www.nlm.nih.gov/research/visible/visible_human.html

While all of the above references may be of interest to physicians who study and treat apraxia, the following are particularly noteworthy.

The NLM Gateway[23]

The NLM (National Library of Medicine) Gateway is a Web-based system that lets users search simultaneously in multiple retrieval systems at the U.S. National Library of Medicine (NLM). It allows users of NLM services to initiate searches from one Web interface, providing "one-stop searching" for many of NLM's information resources or databases.[24] One target audience for the Gateway is the Internet user who is new to NLM's online resources and does not know what information is available or how best to search for it. This audience may include physicians and other healthcare providers,

---

[23] Adapted from NLM: **http://gateway.nlm.nih.gov/gw/Cmd?Overview.x**.
[24] The NLM Gateway is currently being developed by the Lister Hill National Center for Biomedical Communications (LHNCBC) at the National Library of Medicine (NLM) of the National Institutes of Health (NIH).

researchers, librarians, students, and, increasingly, patients, their families, and the public.[25] To use the NLM Gateway, simply go to the search site at **http://gateway.nlm.nih.gov/gw/Cmd**. Type "apraxia" (or synonyms) into the search box and click "Search." The results will be presented in a tabular form, indicating the number of references in each database category.

Results Summary

Category	Items Found
Journal Articles	347458
Books / Periodicals / Audio Visual	2573
Consumer Health	294
Meeting Abstracts	3093
Other Collections	100
Total	353518

HSTAT[26]

HSTAT is a free, Web-based resource that provides access to full-text documents used in healthcare decision-making.[27] HSTAT's audience includes healthcare providers, health service researchers, policy makers, insurance companies, consumers, and the information professionals who serve these groups. HSTAT provides access to a wide variety of publications, including clinical practice guidelines, quick-reference guides for clinicians, consumer health brochures, evidence reports and technology assessments from the Agency for Healthcare Research and Quality (AHRQ), as well as AHRQ's Put Prevention Into Practice.[28] Simply search by "apraxia" (or synonyms) at the following Web site: **http://text.nlm.nih.gov**.

[25] Other users may find the Gateway useful for an overall search of NLM's information resources. Some searchers may locate what they need immediately, while others will utilize the Gateway as an adjunct tool to other NLM search services such as PubMed® and MEDLINEplus®. The Gateway connects users with multiple NLM retrieval systems while also providing a search interface for its own collections. These collections include various types of information that do not logically belong in PubMed, LOCATORplus, or other established NLM retrieval systems (e.g., meeting announcements and pre-1966 journal citations). The Gateway will provide access to the information found in an increasing number of NLM retrieval systems in several phases.

[26] Adapted from HSTAT: **http://www.nlm.nih.gov/pubs/factsheets/hstat.html**

[27] The HSTAT URL is **http://hstat.nlm.nih.gov/**.

[28] Other important documents in HSTAT include: the National Institutes of Health (NIH) Consensus Conference Reports and Technology Assessment Reports; the HIV/AIDS Treatment Information Service (ATIS) resource documents; the Substance Abuse and Mental Health Services Administration's Center for Substance Abuse Treatment (SAMHSA/CSAT)

Coffee Break: Tutorials for Biologists[29]

Some patients may wish to have access to a general healthcare site that takes a scientific view of the news and covers recent breakthroughs in biology that may one day assist physicians in developing treatments. To this end, we recommend "Coffee Break," a collection of short reports on recent biological discoveries. Each report incorporates interactive tutorials that demonstrate how bioinformatics tools are used as a part of the research process. Currently, all Coffee Breaks are written by NCBI staff.[30] Each report is about 400 words and is usually based on a discovery reported in one or more articles from recently published, peer-reviewed literature.[31] This site has new articles every few weeks, so it can be considered an online magazine of sorts, and intended for general background information. You can access the Coffee Break Web site at **http://www.ncbi.nlm.nih.gov/Coffeebreak/**.

Other Commercial Databases

In addition to resources maintained by official agencies, other databases exist that are commercial ventures addressing medical professionals. Here are a few examples that may interest you:

- **CliniWeb International:** Index and table of contents to selected clinical information on the Internet; see **http://www.ohsu.edu/cliniweb/**.

- **Image Engine:** Multimedia electronic medical record system that integrates a wide range of digitized clinical images with textual data stored in the University of Pittsburgh Medical Center's MARS electronic medical record system; see the following Web site: **http://www.cml.upmc.edu/cml/imageengine/imageEngine.html**.

Treatment Improvement Protocols (TIP) and Center for Substance Abuse Prevention (SAMHSA/CSAP) Prevention Enhancement Protocols System (PEPS); the Public Health Service (PHS) Preventive Services Task Force's *Guide to Clinical Preventive Services*; the independent, nonfederal Task Force on Community Services *Guide to Community Preventive Services*; and the Health Technology Advisory Committee (HTAC) of the Minnesota Health Care Commission (MHCC) health technology evaluations.

[29] Adapted from **http://www.ncbi.nlm.nih.gov/Coffeebreak/Archive/FAQ.html**

[30] The figure that accompanies each article is frequently supplied by an expert external to NCBI, in which case the source of the figure is cited. The result is an interactive tutorial that tells a biological story.

[31] After a brief introduction that sets the work described into a broader context, the report focuses on how a molecular understanding can provide explanations of observed biology and lead to therapies for diseases. Each vignette is accompanied by a figure and hypertext links that lead to a series of pages that interactively show how NCBI tools and resources are used in the research process.

- **Medical World Search:** Searches full text from thousands of selected medical sites on the Internet; see **http://www.mwsearch.com/**.

- **MedWeaver:** Prototype system that allows users to search differential diagnoses for any list of signs and symptoms, to search medical literature, and to explore relevant Web sites; see **http://www.med.virginia.edu/~wmd4n/medweaver.html**.

- **Metaphrase:** Middleware component intended for use by both caregivers and medical records personnel. It converts the informal language generally used by caregivers into terms from formal, controlled vocabularies; see the following Web site: **http://www.lexical.com/Metaphrase.html**.

The Genome Project and Apraxia

With all the discussion in the press about the Human Genome Project, it is only natural that physicians, researchers, and patients want to know about how human genes relate to apraxia. In the following section, we will discuss databases and references used by physicians and scientists who work in this area.

Online Mendelian Inheritance in Man (OMIM)

The Online Mendelian Inheritance in Man (OMIM) database is a catalog of human genes and genetic disorders authored and edited by Dr. Victor A. McKusick and his colleagues at Johns Hopkins and elsewhere. OMIM was developed for the World Wide Web by the National Center for Biotechnology Information (NCBI).[32] The database contains textual information, pictures, and reference information. It also contains copious links to NCBI's Entrez database of MEDLINE articles and sequence information.

Go to **http://www.ncbi.nlm.nih.gov/Omim/searchomim.html** to search the database. Type "apraxia" (or synonyms) in the search box, and click "Submit Search." If too many results appear, you can narrow the search by adding the word "clinical." Each report will have additional links to related research

---

[32] Adapted from **http://www.ncbi.nlm.nih.gov/**. Established in 1988 as a national resource for molecular biology information, NCBI creates public databases, conducts research in computational biology, develops software tools for analyzing genome data, and disseminates biomedical information--all for the better understanding of molecular processes affecting human health and disease.

and databases. By following these links, especially the link titled "Database Links," you will be exposed to numerous specialized databases that are largely used by the scientific community. These databases are overly technical and seldom used by the general public, but offer an abundance of information. The following is an example of the results you can obtain from the OMIM for apraxia:

- **Apraxia of Eyelid Opening**
  Web site: http://www.ncbi.nlm.nih.gov/htbin-post/Omim/dispmim?603119

- **Ataxia-oculomotor Apraxia Syndrome**
  Web site: http://www.ncbi.nlm.nih.gov/htbin-post/Omim/dispmim?208920

- **Ocular Motor Apraxia**
  Web site: http://www.ncbi.nlm.nih.gov/htbin-post/Omim/dispmim?257550

Genes and Disease (NCBI - Map)

The Genes and Disease database is produced by the National Center for Biotechnology Information of the National Library of Medicine at the National Institutes of Health. This Web site categorizes each disorder by the system of the body associated with it. Go to http://www.ncbi.nlm.nih.gov/disease/, and browse the system pages to have a full view of important conditions linked to human genes. Since this site is regularly updated, you may wish to re-visit it from time to time. The following systems and associated disorders are addressed:

- **Muscle and Bone:** Movement and growth.
  Examples: Duchenne muscular dystrophy, Ellis-van Creveld syndrome, Marfan syndrome, myotonic dystrophy, spinal muscular atrophy.
  Web site: **http://www.ncbi.nlm.nih.gov/disease/Muscle.html**

- **Nervous System:** Mind and body.
  Examples: Alzheimer disease, Amyotrophic lateral sclerosis, Angelman syndrome, Charcot-Marie-Tooth disease, epilepsy, essential tremor, Fragile X syndrome, Friedreich's ataxia, Huntington disease, Niemann-Pick disease, Parkinson disease, Prader-Willi syndrome, Rett syndrome, Spinocerebellar atrophy, Williams syndrome.
  Web site: **http://www.ncbi.nlm.nih.gov/disease/Brain.html**

- **Signals:** Cellular messages.
  Examples: Ataxia telangiectasia, Baldness, Cockayne syndrome,

Glaucoma, SRY: sex determination, Tuberous sclerosis, Waardenburg syndrome, Werner syndrome.
Web site: **http://www.ncbi.nlm.nih.gov/disease/Signals.html**

Entrez

Entrez is a search and retrieval system that integrates several linked databases at the National Center for Biotechnology Information (NCBI). These databases include nucleotide sequences, protein sequences, macromolecular structures, whole genomes, and MEDLINE through PubMed. Entrez provides access to the following databases:

- **PubMed:** Biomedical literature (PubMed),
  Web site: **http://www.ncbi.nlm.nih.gov/entrez/query.fcgi?db=PubMed**

- **Nucleotide Sequence Database (Genbank):**
  Web site:
  http://www.ncbi.nlm.nih.gov/entrez/query.fcgi?db=Nucleotide

- **Protein Sequence Database:**
  Web site: **http://www.ncbi.nlm.nih.gov/entrez/query.fcgi?db=Protein**

- **Structure:** Three-dimensional macromolecular structures,
  Web site: **http://www.ncbi.nlm.nih.gov/entrez/query.fcgi?db=Structure**

- **Genome:** Complete genome assemblies,
  Web site: **http://www.ncbi.nlm.nih.gov/entrez/query.fcgi?db=Genome**

- **PopSet:** Population study data sets,
  Web site: **http://www.ncbi.nlm.nih.gov/entrez/query.fcgi?db=Popset**

- **OMIM:** Online Mendelian Inheritance in Man,
  Web site: **http://www.ncbi.nlm.nih.gov/entrez/query.fcgi?db=OMIM**

- **Taxonomy:** Organisms in GenBank,
  Web site:
  http://www.ncbi.nlm.nih.gov/entrez/query.fcgi?db=Taxonomy

- **Books:** Online books,
  Web site: **http://www.ncbi.nlm.nih.gov/entrez/query.fcgi?db=books**

- **ProbeSet:** Gene Expression Omnibus (GEO),
  Web site: **http://www.ncbi.nlm.nih.gov/entrez/query.fcgi?db=geo**

- **3D Domains:** Domains from Entrez Structure,
  Web site: **http://www.ncbi.nlm.nih.gov/entrez/query.fcgi?db=geo**

- **NCBI's Protein Sequence Information Survey Results:**
  Web site: **http://www.ncbi.nlm.nih.gov/About/proteinsurvey/**

To access the Entrez system at the National Center for Biotechnology Information, go to **http://www.ncbi.nlm.nih.gov/entrez**, and then select the database that you would like to search. The databases available are listed in the drop box next to "Search." In the box next to "for," enter "apraxia" (or synonyms) and click "Go."

Jablonski's Multiple Congenital Anomaly/Mental Retardation (MCA/MR) Syndromes Database[33]

This online resource can be quite useful. It has been developed to facilitate the identification and differentiation of syndromic entities. Special attention is given to the type of information that is usually limited or completely omitted in existing reference sources due to space limitations of the printed form.

At the following Web site you can also search across syndromes using an index: **http://www.nlm.nih.gov/mesh/jablonski/syndrome_toc/toc_a.html.** You can search by keywords at this Web site: **http://www.nlm.nih.gov/mesh/jablonski/syndrome_db.html**.

The Genome Database[34]

Established at Johns Hopkins University in Baltimore, Maryland in 1990, the Genome Database (GDB) is the official central repository for genomic mapping data resulting from the Human Genome Initiative. In the spring of 1999, the Bioinformatics Supercomputing Centre (BiSC) at the Hospital for Sick Children in Toronto, Ontario assumed the management of GDB. The Human Genome Initiative is a worldwide research effort focusing on structural analysis of human DNA to determine the location and sequence of the estimated 100,000 human genes. In support of this project, GDB stores and curates data generated by researchers worldwide who are engaged in the mapping effort of the Human Genome Project (HGP). GDB's mission is to provide scientists with an encyclopedia of the human genome which is continually revised and updated to reflect the current state of scientific knowledge. Although GDB has historically focused on gene mapping, its focus will broaden as the Genome Project moves from mapping to sequence, and finally, to functional analysis.

---

[33] Adapted from the National Library of Medicine:
http://www.nlm.nih.gov/mesh/jablonski/about_syndrome.html.
[34] Adapted from the Genome Database:
http://gdbwww.gdb.org/gdb/aboutGDB.html#mission.

To access the GDB, simply go to the following hyperlink: **http://www.gdb.org/**. Search "All Biological Data" by "Keyword." Type "apraxia" (or synonyms) into the search box, and review the results. If more than one word is used in the search box, then separate each one with the word "and" or "or" (using "or" might be useful when using synonyms). This database is extremely technical as it was created for specialists. The articles are the results which are the most accessible to non-professionals and often listed under the heading "Citations." The contact names are also accessible to non-professionals.

Specialized References

The following books are specialized references written for professionals interested in apraxia (sorted alphabetically by title, hyperlinks provide rankings, information, and reviews at Amazon.com):

- **The Behavioral Neurology of White Matter** by Christopher M. Filley; Paperback - 279 pages; 1st edition (September 15, 2001), Oxford University Press; ISBN: 019513561X;
  http://www.amazon.com/exec/obidos/ASIN/019513561X/icongroupinterna

- **The Cerebellum and Its Disorders** by Mario-Ubaldo Manto, Massimo Pandolfo; Hardcover - 1st edition (January 2002), Cambridge University Press; ISBN: 0521771560;
  http://www.amazon.com/exec/obidos/ASIN/0521771560/icongroupinterna

- **Clinical Neurology** by David A. Greenberg, et al; Paperback - 390 pages; 5th edition (February 9, 2002), Appleton & Lange; ISBN: 0071375430;
  http://www.amazon.com/exec/obidos/ASIN/0071375430/icongroupinterna

- **Clinical Neurology for Psychiatrists** by David M. Kaufman; Hardcover - 670 pages, 5th edition (January 15, 2001), W. B. Saunders Co.; ISBN: 0721689957;
  http://www.amazon.com/exec/obidos/ASIN/0721689957/icongroupinterna

- **Comprehensive Neurology** by Roger N. Rosenberg (Editor), David E. Pleasure (Editor); 1280 pages, 2nd edition (April 1998), Wiley-Liss; ISBN: 0471169587;
  http://www.amazon.com/exec/obidos/ASIN/0471169587/icongroupinterna

- **Emergent and Urgent Neurology** by William J. Weiner (Editor), Lisa M. Shulman (Editor); Hardcover - 571 pages; 2nd edition (January 15, 1999), Lippincott, Williams & Wilkins Publishers; ISBN: 0397518579;
  http://www.amazon.com/exec/obidos/ASIN/0397518579/icongroupinterna

- **Neurology in Clinical Practice: Volume I: Principles of Diagnosis and Management, Volume II: The Neurological Disorders (2-Volume Set, Includes a 12-Month Subscription to the Online Edition)** by W. G. Bradley, et al; Hardcover - 2413 pages, 3rd edition, Vol 1-2 (January 15, 2000), Butterworth-Heinemann; ISBN: 0750699736; http://www.amazon.com/exec/obidos/ASIN/0750699736/icongroupinterna

- **Neuroscience: Exploring the Brain** by Mark F. Bear, et al; Hardcover - 855 pages, 2nd edition (January 15, 2001), Lippincott, Williams & Wilkins Publishers; ISBN: 0683305964; http://www.amazon.com/exec/obidos/ASIN/0683305964/icongroupinterna

- **Office Practice of Neurology** by Martain A. Samuels, Steven F. Feske; Hardcover, Churchill Livingstone; ISBN: 0443065578; http://www.amazon.com/exec/obidos/ASIN/0443065578/icongroupinterna

- **Patient-Based Approaches to Cognitive Neuroscience** by Martha J. Farah (Editor), Todd E. Feinberg (Editor); Paperback - 425 pages (April 3, 2000), MIT Press; ISBN: 0262561239; http://www.amazon.com/exec/obidos/ASIN/0262561239/icongroupinterna

- **Principles of Neural Science** by Eric R. Kandel (Editor), et al; Hardcover - 1414 pages, 4th edition (January 5, 2000), McGraw-Hill Professional Publishing; ISBN: 0838577016; http://www.amazon.com/exec/obidos/ASIN/0838577016/icongroupinterna

- **Review Manual for Neurology in Clinical Practice** by Karl E. Misulis, et al; Paperback, Butterworth-Heinemann Medical; ISBN: 0750671920; http://www.amazon.com/exec/obidos/ASIN/0750671920/icongroupinterna

Vocabulary Builder

Cerebellum: Part of the metencephalon that lies in the posterior cranial fossa behind the brain stem. It is concerned with the coordination of movement. [NIH]

CHAPTER 9. DISSERTATIONS ON APRAXIA

Overview

University researchers are active in studying almost all known diseases. The result of research is often published in the form of Doctoral or Master's dissertations. You should understand, therefore, that applied diagnostic procedures and/or therapies can take many years to develop after the thesis that proposed the new technique or approach was written.

In this chapter, we will give you a bibliography on recent dissertations relating to apraxia. You can read about these in more detail using the Internet or your local medical library. We will also provide you with information on how to use the Internet to stay current on dissertations.

Dissertations on Apraxia

ProQuest Digital Dissertations is the largest archive of academic dissertations available. From this archive, we have compiled the following list covering dissertations devoted to apraxia. You will see that the information provided includes the dissertation's title, its author, and the author's institution. To read more about the following, simply use the Internet address indicated. The following covers recent dissertations dealing with apraxia:

- **Distinctive Error Profiles and Segmental Inconsistency Within Developmental Verbal/speech Apraxia** by Shelton, Julie Owen; Phd from The University of Oklahoma Health Sciences Center, 2002, 204 pages
  http://wwwlib.umi.com/dissertations/fullcit/3041174

- **Manual Dexterity and Developmental Verbal Apraxia in Young Children.** by Kornse, Diane D., Edd from Lehigh University, 1978, 99 pages
  http://wwwlib.umi.com/dissertations/fullcit/7908512

- **Temporal Patterning of Aerodynamic and Acoustic Events in Apraxia of Speech** by Dodaro, Robert Raymond, Phd from The University of Michigan, 1987, 254 pages
  http://wwwlib.umi.com/dissertations/fullcit/8712098

- **The Description and Comparison of Feature Retention Patterns for Children with Phonological Impairment, Developmental Apraxia of Speech, and Typically Developing Children** by Lambert, Amanda Nicole; Ms from East Tennessee State University, 2001, 67 pages
  http://wwwlib.umi.com/dissertations/fullcit/1404107

Keeping Current

As previously mentioned, an effective way to stay current on dissertations dedicated to apraxia is to use the database called *ProQuest Digital Dissertations* via the Internet, located at the following Web address: **http://wwwlib.umi.com/dissertations.** The site allows you to freely access the last two years of citations and abstracts. Ask your medical librarian if the library has full and unlimited access to this database. From the library, you should be able to do more complete searches than with the limited 2-year access available to the general public.

PART III. APPENDICES

ABOUT PART III

Part III is a collection of appendices on general medical topics which may be of interest to patients with apraxia and related conditions.

APPENDIX A. RESEARCHING YOUR MEDICATIONS

Overview

There are a number of sources available on new or existing medications which could be prescribed to patients with apraxia. While a number of hard copy or CD-Rom resources are available to patients and physicians for research purposes, a more flexible method is to use Internet-based databases. In this chapter, we will begin with a general overview of medications. We will then proceed to outline official recommendations on how you should view your medications. You may also want to research medications that you are currently taking for other conditions as they may interact with medications for apraxia. Research can give you information on the side effects, interactions, and limitations of prescription drugs used in the treatment of apraxia. Broadly speaking, there are two sources of information on approved medications: public sources and private sources. We will emphasize free-to-use public sources.

Your Medications: The Basics[35]

The Agency for Health Care Research and Quality has published extremely useful guidelines on how you can best participate in the medication aspects of apraxia. Taking medicines is not always as simple as swallowing a pill. It can involve many steps and decisions each day. The AHCRQ recommends that patients with apraxia take part in treatment decisions. Do not be afraid to ask questions and talk about your concerns. By taking a moment to ask questions early, you may avoid problems later. Here are some points to cover each time a new medicine is prescribed:

- Ask about all parts of your treatment, including diet changes, exercise, and medicines.

- Ask about the risks and benefits of each medicine or other treatment you might receive.

- Ask how often you or your doctor will check for side effects from a given medication.

Do not hesitate to ask what is important to you about your medicines. You may want a medicine with the fewest side effects, or the fewest doses to take each day. You may care most about cost, or how the medicine might affect how you live or work. Or, you may want the medicine your doctor believes will work the best. Telling your doctor will help him or her select the best treatment for you.

Do not be afraid to "bother" your doctor with your concerns and questions about medications for apraxia. You can also talk to a nurse or a pharmacist. They can help you better understand your treatment plan. Feel free to bring a friend or family member with you when you visit your doctor. Talking over your options with someone you trust can help you make better choices, especially if you are not feeling well. Specifically, ask your doctor the following:

- The name of the medicine and what it is supposed to do.

- How and when to take the medicine, how much to take, and for how long.

- What food, drinks, other medicines, or activities you should avoid while taking the medicine.

- What side effects the medicine may have, and what to do if they occur.

- If you can get a refill, and how often.

---

[35] This section is adapted from AHCRQ: **http://www.ahcpr.gov/consumer/ncpiebro.htm** .

- About any terms or directions you do not understand.

- What to do if you miss a dose.

- If there is written information you can take home (most pharmacies have information sheets on your prescription medicines; some even offer large-print or Spanish versions).

Do not forget to tell your doctor about all the medicines you are currently taking (not just those for apraxia). This includes prescription medicines and the medicines that you buy over the counter. Then your doctor can avoid giving you a new medicine that may not work well with the medications you take now. When talking to your doctor, you may wish to prepare a list of medicines you currently take, the reason you take them, and how you take them. Be sure to include the following information for each:

- Name of medicine

- Reason taken

- Dosage

- Time(s) of day

Also include any over-the-counter medicines, such as:

- Laxatives

- Diet pills

- Vitamins

- Cold medicine

- Aspirin or other pain, headache, or fever medicine

- Cough medicine

- Allergy relief medicine

- Antacids

- Sleeping pills

- Others (include names)

Learning More about Your Medications

Because of historical investments by various organizations and the emergence of the Internet, it has become rather simple to learn about the medications your doctor has recommended for apraxia. One such source is the United States Pharmacopeia. In 1820, eleven physicians met in Washington, D.C. to establish the first compendium of standard drugs for the United States. They called this compendium the "U.S. Pharmacopeia (USP)." Today, the USP is a non-profit organization consisting of 800 volunteer scientists, eleven elected officials, and 400 representatives of state associations and colleges of medicine and pharmacy. The USP is located in Rockville, Maryland, and its home page is located at **www.usp.org**. The USP currently provides standards for over 3,700 medications. The resulting USP DI® Advice for the Patient® can be accessed through the National Library of Medicine of the National Institutes of Health. The database is partially derived from lists of federally approved medications in the Food and Drug Administration's (FDA) Drug Approvals database.[36]

While the FDA database is rather large and difficult to navigate, the Phamacopeia is both user-friendly and free to use. It covers more than 9,000 prescription and over-the-counter medications. To access this database, simply type the following hyperlink into your Web browser: **http://www.nlm.nih.gov/medlineplus/druginformation.html**. To view examples of a given medication (brand names, category, description, preparation, proper use, precautions, side effects, etc.), simply follow the hyperlinks indicated within the United States Pharmacopoeia (USP). It is important to read the disclaimer by the USP (**http://www.nlm.nih.gov/medlineplus/drugdisclaimer.html**) before using the information provided.

Commercial Databases

In addition to the medications listed in the USP above, a number of commercial sites are available by subscription to physicians and their institutions. You may be able to access these sources from your local medical library or your doctor's office.

Reuters Health Drug Database

The Reuters Health Drug Database can be searched by keyword at the hyperlink: **http://www.reutershealth.com/frame2/drug.html**. The following medications are listed in the Reuters' database as associated with apraxia (including those with contraindications):[37]

---

[36] Though cumbersome, the FDA database can be freely browsed at the following site: **www.fda.gov/cder/da/da.htm**.

[37] Adapted from *A to Z Drug Facts* by Facts and Comparisons.

- **Obesity threatens to reverse gains in longevity**
  http://www.reutershealth.com/archive/2002/09/09/eline/links/20020
  909elin034.htm

Mosby's GenRx

Mosby's GenRx database (also available on CD-Rom and book format) covers 45,000 drug products including generics and international brands. It provides prescribing information, drug interactions, and patient information. Information can be obtained at the following hyperlink: **http://www.genrx.com/Mosby/PhyGenRx/group.html.**

Physicians Desk Reference

The Physicians Desk Reference database (also available in CD-Rom and book format) is a full-text drug database. The database is searchable by brand name, generic name or by indication. It features multiple drug interactions reports. Information can be obtained at the following hyperlink: **http://physician.pdr.net/physician/templates/en/acl/psuser_t.htm.**

Other Web Sites

A number of additional Web sites discuss drug information. As an example, you may like to look at **www.drugs.com** which reproduces the information in the Pharmacopeia as well as commercial information. You may also want to consider the Web site of the Medical Letter, Inc. which allows users to download articles on various drugs and therapeutics for a nominal fee: **http://www.medletter.com/.**

Contraindications and Interactions (Hidden Dangers)

Some of the medications mentioned in the previous discussions can be problematic for patients with apraxia--not because they are used in the treatment process, but because of contraindications, or side effects. Medications with contraindications are those that could react with drugs used to treat apraxia or potentially create deleterious side effects in patients with apraxia. You should ask your physician about any contraindications, especially as these might apply to other medications that you may be taking for common ailments.

Drug-drug interactions occur when two or more drugs react with each other. This drug-drug interaction may cause you to experience an unexpected side effect. Drug interactions may make your medications less effective, cause unexpected side effects, or increase the action of a particular drug. Some drug interactions can even be harmful to you.

Be sure to read the label every time you use a nonprescription or prescription drug, and take the time to learn about drug interactions. These precautions may be critical to your health. You can reduce the risk of potentially harmful drug interactions and side effects with a little bit of knowledge and common sense.

Drug labels contain important information about ingredients, uses, warnings, and directions which you should take the time to read and understand. Labels also include warnings about possible drug interactions. Further, drug labels may change as new information becomes available. This is why it's especially important to read the label every time you use a medication. When your doctor prescribes a new drug, discuss all over-the-counter and prescription medications, dietary supplements, vitamins, botanicals, minerals and herbals you take as well as the foods you eat. Ask your pharmacist for the package insert for each prescription drug you take. The package insert provides more information about potential drug interactions.

A Final Warning

At some point, you may hear of alternative medications from friends, relatives, or in the news media. Advertisements may suggest that certain alternative drugs can produce positive results for patients with apraxia. Exercise caution--some of these drugs may have fraudulent claims, and others may actually hurt you. The Food and Drug Administration (FDA) is the official U.S. agency charged with discovering which medications are likely to improve the health of patients with apraxia. The FDA warns patients to watch out for[38]:

- Secret formulas (real scientists share what they know)

---

[38] This section has been adapted from **http://www.fda.gov/opacom/lowlit/medfraud.html**

- Amazing breakthroughs or miracle cures (real breakthroughs don't happen very often; when they do, real scientists do not call them amazing or miracles)

- Quick, painless, or guaranteed cures

- If it sounds too good to be true, it probably isn't true.

If you have any questions about any kind of medical treatment, the FDA may have an office near you. Look for their number in the blue pages of the phone book. You can also contact the FDA through its toll-free number, 1-888-INFO-FDA (1-888-463-6332), or on the World Wide Web at **www.fda.gov**.

General References

In addition to the resources provided earlier in this chapter, the following general references describe medications (sorted alphabetically by title; hyperlinks provide rankings, information and reviews at Amazon.com):

- **Current Therapy in Neurologic Disease** by Richard T. Johnson, et al; Hardcover - 457 pages, 6th edition (January 15, 2002), Mosby-Year Book; ISBN: 0323014720;
  http://www.amazon.com/exec/obidos/ASIN/0323014720/icongroupinterna

- **Emerging Pharmacological Tools in Clinical Neurology** by MedPanel Inc. (Author); Digital - 66 pages, MarketResearch.com; ISBN: B00005RBN8;
  http://www.amazon.com/exec/obidos/ASIN/B00005RBN8/icongroupinterna

- **Goodman & Gilman's The Pharmacological Basis of Therapeutics by** Joel G. Hardman (Editor), Lee E. Limbird; Hardcover - 1825 pages, 10th edition (August 13, 2001), McGraw-Hill Professional Publishing; ISBN: 0071354697;
  http://www.amazon.com/exec/obidos/ASIN/0071354697/icongroupinterna

- **Neurology and General Medicine** by Michael J. Aminoff (Editor), Hardcover - 992 pages, 3rd edition (March 15, 2001), Churchill Livingstone; ISBN: 0443065713;
  http://www.amazon.com/exec/obidos/ASIN/0443065713/icongroupinterna

- **Neurology and Medicine** by Hughes Perkins; Hardcover - 415 pages, 1st edition (December 15, 1999), B. M. J. Books; ISBN: 0727912240;
  http://www.amazon.com/exec/obidos/ASIN/0727912240/icongroupinterna

- **Pharmacological Management of Neurological and Psychiatric Disorders** by S. J. Enna (Editor), et al; Hardcover - 736 pages, 1st edition, McGraw-Hill Professional Publishing; ISBN: 0070217645; http://www.amazon.com/exec/obidos/ASIN/0070217645/icongroupinterna

Vocabulary Builder

The following vocabulary builder gives definitions of words used in this chapter that have not been defined in previous chapters:

Psychiatric: Pertaining to or within the purview of psychiatry. [EU]

APPENDIX B. RESEARCHING ALTERNATIVE MEDICINE

Overview

Complementary and alternative medicine (CAM) is one of the most contentious aspects of modern medical practice. You may have heard of these treatments on the radio or on television. Maybe you have seen articles written about these treatments in magazines, newspapers, or books. Perhaps your friends or doctor have mentioned alternatives.

In this chapter, we will begin by giving you a broad perspective on complementary and alternative therapies. Next, we will introduce you to official information sources on CAM relating to apraxia. Finally, at the conclusion of this chapter, we will provide a list of readings on apraxia from various authors. We will begin, however, with the National Center for Complementary and Alternative Medicine's (NCCAM) overview of complementary and alternative medicine.

What Is CAM?[39]

Complementary and alternative medicine (CAM) covers a broad range of healing philosophies, approaches, and therapies. Generally, it is defined as those treatments and healthcare practices which are not taught in medical schools, used in hospitals, or reimbursed by medical insurance companies. Many CAM therapies are termed "holistic," which generally means that the healthcare practitioner considers the whole person, including physical, mental, emotional, and spiritual health. Some of these therapies are also known as "preventive," which means that the practitioner educates and

---

[39] Adapted from the NCCAM: **http://nccam.nih.gov/nccam/fcp/faq/index.html#what-is**.

treats the person to prevent health problems from arising, rather than treating symptoms after problems have occurred.

People use CAM treatments and therapies in a variety of ways. Therapies are used alone (often referred to as alternative), in combination with other alternative therapies, or in addition to conventional treatment (sometimes referred to as complementary). Complementary and alternative medicine, or "integrative medicine," includes a broad range of healing philosophies, approaches, and therapies. Some approaches are consistent with physiological principles of Western medicine, while others constitute healing systems with non-Western origins. While some therapies are far outside the realm of accepted Western medical theory and practice, others are becoming established in mainstream medicine.

Complementary and alternative therapies are used in an effort to prevent illness, reduce stress, prevent or reduce side effects and symptoms, or control or cure disease. Some commonly used methods of complementary or alternative therapy include mind/body control interventions such as visualization and relaxation, manual healing including acupressure and massage, homeopathy, vitamins or herbal products, and acupuncture.

What Are the Domains of Alternative Medicine?[40]

The list of CAM practices changes continually. The reason being is that these new practices and therapies are often proved to be safe and effective, and therefore become generally accepted as "mainstream" healthcare practices. Today, CAM practices may be grouped within five major domains: (1) alternative medical systems, (2) mind-body interventions, (3) biologically-based treatments, (4) manipulative and body-based methods, and (5) energy therapies. The individual systems and treatments comprising these categories are too numerous to list in this sourcebook. Thus, only limited examples are provided within each.

Alternative Medical Systems

Alternative medical systems involve complete systems of theory and practice that have evolved independent of, and often prior to, conventional biomedical approaches. Many are traditional systems of medicine that are

---

[40] Adapted from the NCCAM: **http://nccam.nih.gov/nccam/fcp/classify/index.html**

practiced by individual cultures throughout the world, including a number of venerable Asian approaches.

Traditional oriental medicine emphasizes the balance or disturbances of qi (pronounced chi) or vital energy in health and disease, respectively. Traditional oriental medicine consists of a group of techniques and methods including acupuncture, herbal medicine, oriental massage, and qi gong (a form of energy therapy). Acupuncture involves stimulating specific anatomic points in the body for therapeutic purposes, usually by puncturing the skin with a thin needle.

Ayurveda is India's traditional system of medicine. Ayurvedic medicine (meaning "science of life") is a comprehensive system of medicine that places equal emphasis on body, mind, and spirit. Ayurveda strives to restore the innate harmony of the individual. Some of the primary Ayurvedic treatments include diet, exercise, meditation, herbs, massage, exposure to sunlight, and controlled breathing.

Other traditional healing systems have been developed by the world's indigenous populations. These populations include Native American, Aboriginal, African, Middle Eastern, Tibetan, and Central and South American cultures. Homeopathy and naturopathy are also examples of complete alternative medicine systems.

Homeopathic medicine is an unconventional Western system that is based on the principle that "like cures like," i.e., that the same substance that in large doses produces the symptoms of an illness, in very minute doses cures it. Homeopathic health practitioners believe that the more dilute the remedy, the greater its potency. Therefore, they use small doses of specially prepared plant extracts and minerals to stimulate the body's defense mechanisms and healing processes in order to treat illness.

Naturopathic medicine is based on the theory that disease is a manifestation of alterations in the processes by which the body naturally heals itself and emphasizes health restoration rather than disease treatment. Naturopathic physicians employ an array of healing practices, including the following: diet and clinical nutrition, homeopathy, acupuncture, herbal medicine, hydrotherapy (the use of water in a range of temperatures and methods of applications), spinal and soft-tissue manipulation, physical therapies (such as those involving electrical currents, ultrasound, and light), therapeutic counseling, and pharmacology.

Mind-Body Interventions

Mind-body interventions employ a variety of techniques designed to facilitate the mind's capacity to affect bodily function and symptoms. Only a select group of mind-body interventions having well-documented theoretical foundations are considered CAM. For example, patient education and cognitive-behavioral approaches are now considered "mainstream." On the other hand, complementary and alternative medicine includes meditation, certain uses of hypnosis, dance, music, and art therapy, as well as prayer and mental healing.

Biological-Based Therapies

This category of CAM includes natural and biological-based practices, interventions, and products, many of which overlap with conventional medicine's use of dietary supplements. This category includes herbal, special dietary, orthomolecular, and individual biological therapies.

Herbal therapy employs an individual herb or a mixture of herbs for healing purposes. An herb is a plant or plant part that produces and contains chemical substances that act upon the body. Special diet therapies, such as those proposed by Drs. Atkins, Ornish, Pritikin, and Weil, are believed to prevent and/or control illness as well as promote health. Orthomolecular therapies aim to treat disease with varying concentrations of chemicals such as magnesium, melatonin, and mega-doses of vitamins. Biological therapies include, for example, the use of laetrile and shark cartilage to treat cancer and the use of bee pollen to treat autoimmune and inflammatory diseases.

Manipulative and Body-Based Methods

This category includes methods that are based on manipulation and/or movement of the body. For example, chiropractors focus on the relationship between structure and function, primarily pertaining to the spine, and how that relationship affects the preservation and restoration of health. Chiropractors use manipulative therapy as an integral treatment tool.

In contrast, osteopaths place particular emphasis on the musculoskeletal system and practice osteopathic manipulation. Osteopaths believe that all of the body's systems work together and that disturbances in one system may have an impact upon function elsewhere in the body. Massage therapists manipulate the soft tissues of the body to normalize those tissues.

Energy Therapies

Energy therapies focus on energy fields originating within the body (biofields) or those from other sources (electromagnetic fields). Biofield therapies are intended to affect energy fields (the existence of which is not yet experimentally proven) that surround and penetrate the human body. Some forms of energy therapy manipulate biofields by applying pressure and/or manipulating the body by placing the hands in or through these fields. Examples include Qi gong, Reiki and Therapeutic Touch.

Qi gong is a component of traditional oriental medicine that combines movement, meditation, and regulation of breathing to enhance the flow of vital energy (qi) in the body, improve blood circulation, and enhance immune function. Reiki, the Japanese word representing Universal Life Energy, is based on the belief that, by channeling spiritual energy through the practitioner, the spirit is healed and, in turn, heals the physical body. Therapeutic Touch is derived from the ancient technique of "laying-on of hands." It is based on the premises that the therapist's healing force affects the patient's recovery and that healing is promoted when the body's energies are in balance. By passing their hands over the patient, these healers identify energy imbalances.

Bioelectromagnetic-based therapies involve the unconventional use of electromagnetic fields to treat illnesses or manage pain. These therapies are often used to treat asthma, cancer, and migraine headaches. Types of electromagnetic fields which are manipulated in these therapies include pulsed fields, magnetic fields, and alternating current or direct current fields.

Can Alternatives Affect My Treatment?

A critical issue in pursuing complementary alternatives mentioned thus far is the risk that these might have undesirable interactions with your medical treatment. It becomes all the more important to speak with your doctor who can offer advice on the use of alternatives. Official sources confirm this view. Though written for women, we find that the National Women's Health Information Center's advice on pursuing alternative medicine is appropriate for patients of both genders and all ages.[41]

---

[41] Adapted from **http://www.4woman.gov/faq/alternative.htm**.

Is It Okay to Want Both Traditional and Alternative or Complementary Medicine?

Should you wish to explore non-traditional types of treatment, be sure to discuss all issues concerning treatments and therapies with your healthcare provider, whether a physician or practitioner of complementary and alternative medicine. Competent healthcare management requires knowledge of both conventional and alternative therapies you are taking for the practitioner to have a complete picture of your treatment plan.

The decision to use complementary and alternative treatments is an important one. Consider before selecting an alternative therapy, the safety and effectiveness of the therapy or treatment, the expertise and qualifications of the healthcare practitioner, and the quality of delivery. These topics should be considered when selecting any practitioner or therapy.

Finding CAM References on Apraxia

Having read the previous discussion, you may be wondering which complementary or alternative treatments might be appropriate for apraxia. For the remainder of this chapter, we will direct you to a number of official sources which can assist you in researching studies and publications. Some of these articles are rather technical, so some patience may be required.

National Center for Complementary and Alternative Medicine

The National Center for Complementary and Alternative Medicine (NCCAM) of the National Institutes of Health (http://nccam.nih.gov) has created a link to the National Library of Medicine's databases to allow patients to search for articles that specifically relate to apraxia and complementary medicine. To search the database, go to the following Web site: **www.nlm.nih.gov/nccam/camonpubmed.html**. Select "CAM on PubMed." Enter "apraxia" (or synonyms) into the search box. Click "Go." The following references provide information on particular aspects of complementary and alternative medicine (CAM) that are related to apraxia:

- **Alien hand syndrome: report of two cases.**
  Author(s): Wu FY, Leong CP, Su TL.
  Source: Changgeng Yi Xue Za Zhi. 1999 December; 22(4): 660-5.
  http://www.ncbi.nlm.nih.gov:80/entrez/query.fcgi?cmd=Retrieve&db=PubMed&list_uids=10695218&dopt=Abstract

- **Bilateral contemporaneous posteroventral pallidotomy for the treatment of Parkinson's disease: neuropsychological and neurological side effects. Report of four cases and review of the literature.**
  Author(s): Ghika J, Ghika-Schmid F, Fankhauser H, Assal G, Vingerhoets F, Albanese A, Bogousslavsky J, Favre J.
  Source: Journal of Neurosurgery. 1999 August; 91(2): 313-21. Review.
  http://www.ncbi.nlm.nih.gov:80/entrez/query.fcgi?cmd=Retrieve&db=PubMed&list_uids=10433321&dopt=Abstract

- **Classical and relational psychology.**
  Author(s): Ectors L.
  Source: Psychotherapy and Psychosomatics. 1970; 18(1): 145-53. No Abstract Available.
  http://www.ncbi.nlm.nih.gov:80/entrez/query.fcgi?cmd=Retrieve&db=PubMed&list_uids=4329252&dopt=Abstract

- **Dark adaptation, motor skills, docosahexaenoic acid, and dyslexia.**
  Author(s): Stordy BJ.
  Source: The American Journal of Clinical Nutrition. 2000 January; 71(1 Suppl): 323S-6S.
  http://www.ncbi.nlm.nih.gov:80/entrez/query.fcgi?cmd=Retrieve&db=PubMed&list_uids=10617990&dopt=Abstract

- **Development of praxis in children.**
  Author(s): Kools JA, Tweedie D.
  Source: Percept Mot Skills. 1975 February; 40(1): 11-9.
  http://www.ncbi.nlm.nih.gov:80/entrez/query.fcgi?cmd=Retrieve&db=PubMed&list_uids=1118249&dopt=Abstract

- **Disorders of perception in stroke.**
  Author(s): Rout MW.
  Source: Age and Ageing. 1978; Suppl: 22-6. No Abstract Available.
  http://www.ncbi.nlm.nih.gov:80/entrez/query.fcgi?cmd=Retrieve&db=PubMed&list_uids=727056&dopt=Abstract

- **Durational changes of apraxic speakers.**
  Author(s): Skenes LL.
  Source: Journal of Communication Disorders. 1987 February; 20(1): 61-71.
  http://www.ncbi.nlm.nih.gov:80/entrez/query.fcgi?cmd=Retrieve&db=PubMed&list_uids=3819004&dopt=Abstract

- **Effect of auditory prestimulation on naming in aphasia.**
  Author(s): Podraza BL, Darley FL.
  Source: Journal of Speech and Hearing Research. 1977 December; 20(4): 669-83.
  http://www.ncbi.nlm.nih.gov:80/entrez/query.fcgi?cmd=Retrieve&db=PubMed&list_uids=604681&dopt=Abstract

- **Electromagnetic articulography treatment for an adult with Broca's aphasia and apraxia of speech.**
  Author(s): Katz WF, Bharadwaj SV, Carstens B.
  Source: Journal of Speech, Language, and Hearing Research : Jslhr. 1999 December; 42(6): 1355-66.
  http://www.ncbi.nlm.nih.gov:80/entrez/query.fcgi?cmd=Retrieve&db=PubMed&list_uids=10599618&dopt=Abstract

- **Identifying, assessing and helping dyspraxic children.**
  Author(s): Flory S.
  Source: Dyslexia (Chichester, England). 2000 July-September; 6(3): 205-8. Review. No Abstract Available.
  http://www.ncbi.nlm.nih.gov:80/entrez/query.fcgi?cmd=Retrieve&db=PubMed&list_uids=10989569&dopt=Abstract

- **Nonverbal dialogue with the brain-damaged elderly.**
  Author(s): Fischer T, Fischer R.
  Source: Confin Psychiatr. 1977; 20(2-3): 61-78.
  http://www.ncbi.nlm.nih.gov:80/entrez/query.fcgi?cmd=Retrieve&db=PubMed&list_uids=923239&dopt=Abstract

- **Normal pressure hydrocephalus.**
  Author(s): Blomerth PR.
  Source: Journal of Manipulative and Physiological Therapeutics. 1993 February; 16(2): 104-6.
  http://www.ncbi.nlm.nih.gov:80/entrez/query.fcgi?cmd=Retrieve&db=PubMed&list_uids=8445351&dopt=Abstract

- **Occupational adaptation: toward a holistic approach for contemporary practice, Part 2.**
  Author(s): Schultz S, Schkade JK.
  Source: Am J Occup Ther. 1992 October; 46(10): 917-25.
  http://www.ncbi.nlm.nih.gov:80/entrez/query.fcgi?cmd=Retrieve&db=PubMed&list_uids=1463064&dopt=Abstract

- **On the different roles of the cerebral hemispheres in mental imagery: the "o'Clock Test" in two clinical cases.**
  Author(s): Grossi D, Modafferi A, Pelosi L, Trojano L.
  Source: Brain and Cognition. 1989 May; 10(1): 18-27.
  http://www.ncbi.nlm.nih.gov:80/entrez/query.fcgi?cmd=Retrieve&db=PubMed&list_uids=2713142&dopt=Abstract

- **Optic aphasia, optic apraxia, and loss of dreaming.**
  Author(s): Pena-Casanova J, Roig-Rovira T, Bermudez A, Tolosa-Sarro E.
  Source: Brain and Language. 1985 September; 26(1): 63-71.
  http://www.ncbi.nlm.nih.gov:80/entrez/query.fcgi?cmd=Retrieve&db=PubMed&list_uids=2413956&dopt=Abstract

- **Patterns of drawing disability in right and left hemispheric patients.**
  Author(s): Gainotti G, Tiacci C.
  Source: Neuropsychologia. 1970 July; 8(3): 379-84. No Abstract Available.
  http://www.ncbi.nlm.nih.gov:80/entrez/query.fcgi?cmd=Retrieve&db=PubMed&list_uids=4941970&dopt=Abstract

- **Progressive impairment of constructional abilities: a visuospatial sketchpad deficit?**
  Author(s): Papagno C.
  Source: Neuropsychologia. 2002; 40(12): 1858.
  http://www.ncbi.nlm.nih.gov:80/entrez/query.fcgi?cmd=Retrieve&db=PubMed&list_uids=12207984&dopt=Abstract

- **Role of somatosensory feedback from tools in realizing movements by patients with ideomotor apraxia.**
  Author(s): Wada Y, Nakagawa Y, Nishikawa T, Aso N, Inokawa M, Kashiwagi A, Tanabe H, Takeda M.
  Source: European Neurology. 1999; 41(2): 73-8.
  http://www.ncbi.nlm.nih.gov:80/entrez/query.fcgi?cmd=Retrieve&db=PubMed&list_uids=10023108&dopt=Abstract

- **Schizokinesis: fragmentation of performance in two strains of pointer dogs.**
  Author(s): Murphree OD, Newton JE.
  Source: Cond Reflex. 1971 April-June; 6(2): 91-100. No Abstract Available.
  http://www.ncbi.nlm.nih.gov:80/entrez/query.fcgi?cmd=Retrieve&db=PubMed&list_uids=5165331&dopt=Abstract

- **Selective deficit of praxis imagery in ideomotor apraxia.**
  Author(s): Ochipa C, Rapcsak SZ, Maher LM, Rothi LJ, Bowers D, Heilman KM.
  Source: Neurology. 1997 August; 49(2): 474-80.
  http://www.ncbi.nlm.nih.gov:80/entrez/query.fcgi?cmd=Retrieve&db=PubMed&list_uids=9270580&dopt=Abstract

- **Singing as therapy for apraxia of speech and aphasia: report of a case.**
  Author(s): Keith RL, Aronson AE.
  Source: Brain and Language. 1975 October; 2(4): 483-8. No Abstract Available.
  http://www.ncbi.nlm.nih.gov:80/entrez/query.fcgi?cmd=Retrieve&db=PubMed&list_uids=1218380&dopt=Abstract

- **The effect of auditory rhythmic stimulation on articulatory accuracy in apraxia of speech.**
  Author(s): Shane HC, Darley FL.
  Source: Cortex. 1978 September; 14(3): 444-50.
  http://www.ncbi.nlm.nih.gov:80/entrez/query.fcgi?cmd=Retrieve&db=PubMed&list_uids=710154&dopt=Abstract

- **The mental representation of hand movements after parietal cortex damage.**
  Author(s): Sirigu A, Duhamel JR, Cohen L, Pillon B, Dubois B, Agid Y.
  Source: Science. 1996 September 13; 273(5281): 1564-8.
  http://www.ncbi.nlm.nih.gov:80/entrez/query.fcgi?cmd=Retrieve&db=PubMed&list_uids=8703221&dopt=Abstract

- **The structure of psychological processes in relation to cerebral organization.**
  Author(s): Luria AR, Simernitskaya EG, Tubylevich B.
  Source: Neuropsychologia. 1970 January; 8(1): 13-9. No Abstract Available.
  http://www.ncbi.nlm.nih.gov:80/entrez/query.fcgi?cmd=Retrieve&db=PubMed&list_uids=5522545&dopt=Abstract

- **The word. A neurologist's view on aphasia.**
  Author(s): Hurwitz LJ.
  Source: Gerontol Clin (Basel). 1971; 13(5): 307-19. No Abstract Available.
  http://www.ncbi.nlm.nih.gov:80/entrez/query.fcgi?cmd=Retrieve&db=PubMed&list_uids=5113982&dopt=Abstract

- **Treatment of acquired aphasia.**
  Author(s): Darley FL.
  Source: Adv Neurol. 1975; 7: 111-45. Review. No Abstract Available.
  http://www.ncbi.nlm.nih.gov:80/entrez/query.fcgi?cmd=Retrieve&db=PubMed&list_uids=1090128&dopt=Abstract

- **Using electropalatography to treat severe acquired apraxia of speech.**
  Author(s): Howard S, Varley R.
  Source: Eur J Disord Commun. 1995; 30(2): 246-55.
  http://www.ncbi.nlm.nih.gov:80/entrez/query.fcgi?cmd=Retrieve&db=PubMed&list_uids=7492855&dopt=Abstract

- **Visuoimaginal constructional apraxia: on a case of selective deficit of imagery.**
  Author(s): Grossi D, Orsini A, Modafferi A, Liotti M.
  Source: Brain and Cognition. 1986 July; 5(3): 255-67.
  http://www.ncbi.nlm.nih.gov:80/entrez/query.fcgi?cmd=Retrieve&db=PubMed&list_uids=3756003&dopt=Abstract

Additional Web Resources

A number of additional Web sites offer encyclopedic information covering CAM and related topics. The following is a representative sample:

- Alternative Medicine Foundation, Inc.: **http://www.herbmed.org/**

- AOL: **http://search.aol.com/cat.adp?id=169&layer=&from=subcats**

- Chinese Medicine: **http://www.newcenturynutrition.com/**

- drkoop.com®:
  http://www.drkoop.com/InteractiveMedicine/IndexC.html

- Family Village: **http://www.familyvillage.wisc.edu/med_altn.htm**

- Google: **http://directory.google.com/Top/Health/Alternative/**

- Healthnotes: **http://www.thedacare.org/healthnotes/**

- Open Directory Project: **http://dmoz.org/Health/Alternative/**

- TPN.com: **http://www.tnp.com/**

- Yahoo.com: **http://dir.yahoo.com/Health/Alternative_Medicine/**

- WebMD®Health: **http://my.webmd.com/drugs_and_herbs**

- WellNet: **http://www.wellnet.ca/herbsa-c.htm**

- WholeHealthMD.com:
  http://www.wholehealthmd.com/reflib/0,1529,,00.html

The following is a specific Web list relating to Apraxia; please note that any particular subject below may indicate either a therapeutic use, or a contraindication (potential danger), and does not reflect an official recommendation:

- **General Overview**

  Apraxia
  Source: Integrative Medicine Communications;
  www.onemedicine.com
  Hyperlink:
  http://www.drkoop.com/InteractiveMedicine/ConsLookups/Symptoms/apraxia.html

- **Alternative Therapy**

  Apraxia
  Source: The Canoe version of A Dictionary of Alternative-Medicine Methods, by Priorities for Health editor Jack Raso, M.S., R.D.
  Hyperlink: http://www.canoe.ca/AltmedDictionary/a.html

General References

A good place to find general background information on CAM is the National Library of Medicine. It has prepared within the MEDLINEplus system an information topic page dedicated to complementary and alternative medicine. To access this page, go to the MEDLINEplus site at: **www.nlm.nih.gov/medlineplus/alternativemedicine.html.** This Web site provides a general overview of various topics and can lead to a number of general sources. The following additional references describe, in broad terms, alternative and complementary medicine (sorted alphabetically by title; hyperlinks provide rankings, information, and reviews at Amazon.com):

- **Alternative and Complementary Treatment in Neurologic Illness** by Michael I. Weintraub (Editor); Paperback - 288 pages (March 23, 2001), Churchill Livingstone; ISBN: 0443065586; http://www.amazon.com/exec/obidos/ASIN/0443065586/icongroupinterna

- **Radical Healing: Integrating the World's Great Therapeutic Traditions to Create a New Transformative Medicine** by Rudolph Ballentine, M.D., Linda Funk (Illustrator); Paperback - 612 pages; Reprint edition (March 14, 2000), Three Rivers Press; ISBN: 0609804847; http://www.amazon.com/exec/obidos/ASIN/0609804847/icongroupinterna

- **The Review of Natural Products** by Facts and Comparisons (Editor); Cd-Rom edition (January 2002), Facts & Comparisons; ISBN: 1574391453; http://www.amazon.com/exec/obidos/ASIN/1574391453/icongroupinterna

For additional information on complementary and alternative medicine, ask your doctor or write to:

> National Institutes of Health
> National Center for Complementary and Alternative Medicine
> Clearinghouse
> P. O. Box 8218
> Silver Spring, MD 20907-8218

Vocabulary Builder

Hydrocephalus: A condition marked by dilatation of the cerebral ventricles, most often occurring secondarily to obstruction of the cerebrospinal fluid pathways, and accompanied by an accumulation of cerebrospinal fluid within the skull; the fluid is usually under increased pressure, but occasionally may be normal or nearly so. It is typically characterized by enlargement of the head, prominence of the forehead, brain atrophy, mental deterioration, and convulsions; may be congenital or acquired; and may be of sudden onset (acute h.) or be slowly progressive (chronic or primary b.). [EU]

Neurosurgery: A surgical specialty concerned with the treatment of diseases and disorders of the brain, spinal cord, and peripheral and sympathetic nervous system. [NIH]

Psychosomatic: Pertaining to the mind-body relationship; having bodily symptoms of psychic, emotional, or mental origin; called also psychophysiologic. [EU]

Psychotherapy: A generic term for the treatment of mental illness or emotional disturbances primarily by verbal or nonverbal communication. [NIH]

APPENDIX C. RESEARCHING NUTRITION

Overview

Since the time of Hippocrates, doctors have understood the importance of diet and nutrition to patients' health and well-being. Since then, they have accumulated an impressive archive of studies and knowledge dedicated to this subject. Based on their experience, doctors and healthcare providers may recommend particular dietary supplements to patients with apraxia. Any dietary recommendation is based on a patient's age, body mass, gender, lifestyle, eating habits, food preferences, and health condition. It is therefore likely that different patients with apraxia may be given different recommendations. Some recommendations may be directly related to apraxia, while others may be more related to the patient's general health. These recommendations, themselves, may differ from what official sources recommend for the average person.

In this chapter we will begin by briefly reviewing the essentials of diet and nutrition that will broadly frame more detailed discussions of apraxia. We will then show you how to find studies dedicated specifically to nutrition and apraxia.

Food and Nutrition: General Principles

What Are Essential Foods?

Food is generally viewed by official sources as consisting of six basic elements: (1) fluids, (2) carbohydrates, (3) protein, (4) fats, (5) vitamins, and (6) minerals. Consuming a combination of these elements is considered to be a healthy diet:

- **Fluids** are essential to human life as 80-percent of the body is composed of water. Water is lost via urination, sweating, diarrhea, vomiting, diuretics (drugs that increase urination), caffeine, and physical exertion.

- **Carbohydrates** are the main source for human energy (thermoregulation) and the bulk of typical diets. They are mostly classified as being either simple or complex. Simple carbohydrates include sugars which are often consumed in the form of cookies, candies, or cakes. Complex carbohydrates consist of starches and dietary fibers. Starches are consumed in the form of pastas, breads, potatoes, rice, and other foods. Soluble fibers can be eaten in the form of certain vegetables, fruits, oats, and legumes. Insoluble fibers include brown rice, whole grains, certain fruits, wheat bran and legumes.

- **Proteins** are eaten to build and repair human tissues. Some foods that are high in protein are also high in fat and calories. Food sources for protein include nuts, meat, fish, cheese, and other dairy products.

- **Fats** are consumed for both energy and the absorption of certain vitamins. There are many types of fats, with many general publications recommending the intake of unsaturated fats or those low in cholesterol.

Vitamins and minerals are fundamental to human health, growth, and, in some cases, disease prevention. Most are consumed in your diet (exceptions being vitamins K and D which are produced by intestinal bacteria and sunlight on the skin, respectively). Each vitamin and mineral plays a different role in health. The following outlines essential vitamins:

- **Vitamin A** is important to the health of your eyes, hair, bones, and skin; sources of vitamin A include foods such as eggs, carrots, and cantaloupe.

- **Vitamin B1**, also known as thiamine, is important for your nervous system and energy production; food sources for thiamine include meat, peas, fortified cereals, bread, and whole grains.

- **Vitamin B2**, also known as riboflavin, is important for your nervous system and muscles, but is also involved in the release of proteins from nutrients; food sources for riboflavin include dairy products, leafy vegetables, meat, and eggs.

- **Vitamin B^3**, also known as niacin, is important for healthy skin and helps the body use energy; food sources for niacin include peas, peanuts, fish, and whole grains

- **Vitamin B^6**, also known as pyridoxine, is important for the regulation of cells in the nervous system and is vital for blood formation; food sources for pyridoxine include bananas, whole grains, meat, and fish.

- **Vitamin B^{12}** is vital for a healthy nervous system and for the growth of red blood cells in bone marrow; food sources for vitamin B^{12} include yeast, milk, fish, eggs, and meat.

- **Vitamin C** allows the body's immune system to fight various diseases, strengthens body tissue, and improves the body's use of iron; food sources for vitamin C include a wide variety of fruits and vegetables.

- **Vitamin D** helps the body absorb calcium which strengthens bones and teeth; food sources for vitamin D include oily fish and dairy products.

- **Vitamin E** can help protect certain organs and tissues from various degenerative diseases; food sources for vitamin E include margarine, vegetables, eggs, and fish.

- **Vitamin K** is essential for bone formation and blood clotting; common food sources for vitamin K include leafy green vegetables.

- **Folic Acid** maintains healthy cells and blood and, when taken by a pregnant woman, can prevent her fetus from developing neural tube defects; food sources for folic acid include nuts, fortified breads, leafy green vegetables, and whole grains.

It should be noted that one can overdose on certain vitamins which become toxic if consumed in excess (e.g. vitamin A, D, E and K).

Like vitamins, minerals are chemicals that are required by the body to remain in good health. Because the human body does not manufacture these chemicals internally, we obtain them from food and other dietary sources. The more important minerals include:

- **Calcium** is needed for healthy bones, teeth, and muscles, but also helps the nervous system function; food sources for calcium include dry beans, peas, eggs, and dairy products.

- **Chromium** is helpful in regulating sugar levels in blood; food sources for chromium include egg yolks, raw sugar, cheese, nuts, beets, whole grains, and meat.

- **Fluoride** is used by the body to help prevent tooth decay and to reinforce bone strength; sources of fluoride include drinking water and certain brands of toothpaste.

- **Iodine** helps regulate the body's use of energy by synthesizing into the hormone thyroxine; food sources include leafy green vegetables, nuts, egg yolks, and red meat.

- **Iron** helps maintain muscles and the formation of red blood cells and certain proteins; food sources for iron include meat, dairy products, eggs, and leafy green vegetables.

- **Magnesium** is important for the production of DNA, as well as for healthy teeth, bones, muscles, and nerves; food sources for magnesium include dried fruit, dark green vegetables, nuts, and seafood.

- **Phosphorous** is used by the body to work with calcium to form bones and teeth; food sources for phosphorous include eggs, meat, cereals, and dairy products.

- **Selenium** primarily helps maintain normal heart and liver functions; food sources for selenium include wholegrain cereals, fish, meat, and dairy products.

- **Zinc** helps wounds heal, the formation of sperm, and encourage rapid growth and energy; food sources include dried beans, shellfish, eggs, and nuts.

The United States government periodically publishes recommended diets and consumption levels of the various elements of food. Again, your doctor may encourage deviations from the average official recommendation based on your specific condition. To learn more about basic dietary guidelines, visit the Web site: **http://www.health.gov/dietaryguidelines/**. Based on these guidelines, many foods are required to list the nutrition levels on the food's packaging. Labeling Requirements are listed at the following site maintained by the Food and Drug Administration: **http://www.cfsan.fda.gov/~dms/lab-cons.html**. When interpreting these requirements, the government recommends that consumers become familiar with the following abbreviations before reading FDA literature:[42]

- **DVs (Daily Values):** A new dietary reference term that will appear on the food label. It is made up of two sets of references, DRVs and RDIs.

- **DRVs (Daily Reference Values):** A set of dietary references that applies to fat, saturated fat, cholesterol, carbohydrate, protein, fiber, sodium, and potassium.

---

[42] Adapted from the FDA: **http://www.fda.gov/fdac/special/foodlabel/dvs.html**.

- **RDIs (Reference Daily Intakes):** A set of dietary references based on the Recommended Dietary Allowances for essential vitamins and minerals and, in selected groups, protein. The name "RDI" replaces the term "U.S. RDA."

- **RDAs (Recommended Dietary Allowances):** A set of estimated nutrient allowances established by the National Academy of Sciences. It is updated periodically to reflect current scientific knowledge.

What Are Dietary Supplements?[43]

Dietary supplements are widely available through many commercial sources, including health food stores, grocery stores, pharmacies, and by mail. Dietary supplements are provided in many forms including tablets, capsules, powders, gel-tabs, extracts, and liquids. Historically in the United States, the most prevalent type of dietary supplement was a multivitamin/mineral tablet or capsule that was available in pharmacies, either by prescription or "over the counter." Supplements containing strictly herbal preparations were less widely available. Currently in the United States, a wide array of supplement products are available, including vitamin, mineral, other nutrients, and botanical supplements as well as ingredients and extracts of animal and plant origin.

The Office of Dietary Supplements (ODS) of the National Institutes of Health is the official agency of the United States which has the expressed goal of acquiring "new knowledge to help prevent, detect, diagnose, and treat disease and disability, from the rarest genetic disorder to the common cold."[44] According to the ODS, dietary supplements can have an important impact on the prevention and management of disease and on the maintenance of health.[45] The ODS notes that considerable research on the effects of dietary supplements has been conducted in Asia and Europe where

---

[43] This discussion has been adapted from the NIH: **http://ods.od.nih.gov/whatare/whatare.html**.

[44] Contact: The Office of Dietary Supplements, National Institutes of Health, Building 31, Room 1B29, 31 Center Drive, MSC 2086, Bethesda, Maryland 20892-2086, Tel: (301) 435-2920, Fax: (301) 480-1845, E-mail: **ods@nih.gov**.

[45] Adapted from **http://ods.od.nih.gov/about/about.html.** The Dietary Supplement Health and Education Act defines dietary supplements as "a product (other than tobacco) intended to supplement the diet that bears or contains one or more of the following dietary ingredients: a vitamin, mineral, amino acid, herb or other botanical; or a dietary substance for use to supplement the diet by increasing the total dietary intake; or a concentrate, metabolite, constituent, extract, or combination of any ingredient described above; and intended for ingestion in the form of a capsule, powder, softgel, or gelcap, and not represented as a conventional food or as a sole item of a meal or the diet."

the use of plant products, in particular, has a long tradition. However, the overwhelming majority of supplements have not been studied scientifically. To explore the role of dietary supplements in the improvement of health care, the ODS plans, organizes, and supports conferences, workshops, and symposia on scientific topics related to dietary supplements. The ODS often works in conjunction with other NIH Institutes and Centers, other government agencies, professional organizations, and public advocacy groups.

To learn more about official information on dietary supplements, visit the ODS site at **http://ods.od.nih.gov/whatare/whatare.html**. Or contact:

> The Office of Dietary Supplements
> National Institutes of Health
> Building 31, Room 1B29
> 31 Center Drive, MSC 2086
> Bethesda, Maryland 20892-2086
> Tel: (301) 435-2920
> Fax: (301) 480-1845
> E-mail: ods@nih.gov

Finding Studies on Apraxia

The NIH maintains an office dedicated to patient nutrition and diet. The National Institutes of Health's Office of Dietary Supplements (ODS) offers a searchable bibliographic database called the IBIDS (International Bibliographic Information on Dietary Supplements). The IBIDS contains over 460,000 scientific citations and summaries about dietary supplements and nutrition as well as references to published international, scientific literature on dietary supplements such as vitamins, minerals, and botanicals.[46] IBIDS is available to the public free of charge through the ODS Internet page: **http://ods.od.nih.gov/databases/ibids.html**.

After entering the search area, you have three choices: (1) IBIDS Consumer Database, (2) Full IBIDS Database, or (3) Peer Reviewed Citations Only. We recommend that you start with the Consumer Database. While you may not find references for the topics that are of most interest to you, check back

---

[46] Adapted from **http://ods.od.nih.gov**. IBIDS is produced by the Office of Dietary Supplements (ODS) at the National Institutes of Health to assist the public, healthcare providers, educators, and researchers in locating credible, scientific information on dietary supplements. IBIDS was developed and will be maintained through an interagency partnership with the Food and Nutrition Information Center of the National Agricultural Library, U.S. Department of Agriculture.

periodically as this database is frequently updated. More studies can be found by searching the Full IBIDS Database. Healthcare professionals and researchers generally use the third option, which lists peer-reviewed citations. In all cases, we suggest that you take advantage of the "Advanced Search" option that allows you to retrieve up to 100 fully explained references in a comprehensive format. Type "apraxia" (or synonyms) into the search box. To narrow the search, you can also select the "Title" field.

The following information is typical of that found when using the "Full IBIDS Database" when searching using "apraxia" (or a synonym):

- "Apraxia of eyelid opening" induced by levodopa therapy and apomorphine in atypical parkinsonism (possible progressive supranuclear palsy): a case report.
  Author(s): Department of Neurological and Psychiatric Sciences, University of Bari, Italy.
  Source: Defazio, G De Mari, M De Salvia, R Lamberti, P Giorelli, M Livrea, P Clin-Neuropharmacol. 1999 Sep-October; 22(5): 292-4 0362-5664

- Lid-opening apraxia in Wilson's disease.
  Author(s): Department of Neurology, LAC/USC Medical Center.
  Source: Keane, J R J-Clin-Neuroophthalmol. 1988 March; 8(1): 31-3 0272-846X

- L-threo-3,4-dihydroxyphenylserine treatment for gait apraxia in parkinsonian patients.
  Source: Yoshida, M Noguchi, S Kuramoto, S Kurume-Med-J. 1989; 36(2): 67-74 0023-5679

- Phenobarbital-induced buccolingual dyskinesia in oral apraxia.
  Author(s): Department of Neurology, University of Sassari, Italy.
  Source: Sechi, G P Piras, M R Rosati, G Zuddas, M Ortu, R Tanca, S Agnetti, V Eur-Neurol. 1988; 28(3): 139-41 0014-3022

Federal Resources on Nutrition

In addition to the IBIDS, the United States Department of Health and Human Services (HHS) and the United States Department of Agriculture (USDA) provide many sources of information on general nutrition and health. Recommended resources include:

- healthfinder®, HHS's gateway to health information, including diet and nutrition:
  http://www.healthfinder.gov/scripts/SearchContext.asp?topic=238&page=0

- The United States Department of Agriculture's Web site dedicated to nutrition information: **www.nutrition.gov**

- The Food and Drug Administration's Web site for federal food safety information: **www.foodsafety.gov**

- The National Action Plan on Overweight and Obesity sponsored by the United States Surgeon General: **http://www.surgeongeneral.gov/topics/obesity/**

- The Center for Food Safety and Applied Nutrition has an Internet site sponsored by the Food and Drug Administration and the Department of Health and Human Services: **http://vm.cfsan.fda.gov/**

- Center for Nutrition Policy and Promotion sponsored by the United States Department of Agriculture: **http://www.usda.gov/cnpp/**

- Food and Nutrition Information Center, National Agricultural Library sponsored by the United States Department of Agriculture: **http://www.nal.usda.gov/fnic/**

- Food and Nutrition Service sponsored by the United States Department of Agriculture: **http://www.fns.usda.gov/fns/**

Additional Web Resources

A number of additional Web sites offer encyclopedic information covering food and nutrition. The following is a representative sample:

- AOL: **http://search.aol.com/cat.adp?id=174&layer=&from=subcats**

- Family Village: **http://www.familyvillage.wisc.edu/med_nutrition.html**

- Google: **http://directory.google.com/Top/Health/Nutrition/**

- Healthnotes: **http://www.thedacare.org/healthnotes/**

- Open Directory Project: **http://dmoz.org/Health/Nutrition/**

- Yahoo.com: **http://dir.yahoo.com/Health/Nutrition/**

- WebMD®Health: **http://my.webmd.com/nutrition**

- WholeHealthMD.com: **http://www.wholehealthmd.com/reflib/0,1529,,00.html**

Vocabulary Builder

The following vocabulary builder defines words used in the references in this chapter that have not been defined in previous chapters:

Apomorphine: A derivative of morphine that is a dopamine D2 agonist. It is a powerful emetic and has been used for that effect in acute poisoning. It has also been used in the diagnosis and treatment of parkinsonism, but its adverse effects limit its use. [NIH]

Atypical: Irregular; not conformable to the type; in microbiology, applied specifically to strains of unusual type. [EU]

Bacteria: Unicellular prokaryotic microorganisms which generally possess rigid cell walls, multiply by cell division, and exhibit three principal forms: round or coccal, rodlike or bacillary, and spiral or spirochetal. [NIH]

Capsules: Hard or soft soluble containers used for the oral administration of medicine. [NIH]

Carbohydrate: An aldehyde or ketone derivative of a polyhydric alcohol, particularly of the pentahydric and hexahydric alcohols. They are so named because the hydrogen and oxygen are usually in the proportion to form water, $(CH_2O)n$. The most important carbohydrates are the starches, sugars, celluloses, and gums. They are classified into mono-, di-, tri-, poly- and heterosaccharides. [EU]

Cholesterol: The principal sterol of all higher animals, distributed in body tissues, especially the brain and spinal cord, and in animal fats and oils. [NIH]

Diarrhea: Passage of excessively liquid or excessively frequent stools. [NIH]

Dyskinesia: Impairment of the power of voluntary movement, resulting in fragmentary or incomplete movements. [EU]

Intestinal: Pertaining to the intestine. [EU]

Iodine: A nonmetallic element of the halogen group that is represented by the atomic symbol I, atomic number 53, and atomic weight of 126.90. It is a nutritionally essential element, especially important in thyroid hormone synthesis. In solution, it has anti-infective properties and is used topically. [NIH]

Levodopa: The naturally occurring form of dopa and the immediate precursor of dopamine. Unlike dopamine itself, it can be taken orally and crosses the blood-brain barrier. It is rapidly taken up by dopaminergic neurons and converted to dopamine. It is used for the treatment of parkinsonism and is usually given with agents that inhibit its conversion to dopamine outside of the central nervous system. [NIH]

Niacin: Water-soluble vitamin of the B complex occurring in various animal and plant tissues. Required by the body for the formation of coenzymes NAD and NADP. Has pellagra-curative, vasodilating, and antilipemic properties. [NIH]

Overdose: 1. to administer an excessive dose. 2. an excessive dose. [EU]

Parkinsonism: A group of neurological disorders characterized by hypokinesia, tremor, and muscular rigidity. [EU]

Phenobarbital: A barbituric acid derivative that acts as a nonselective central nervous system depressant. It promotes binding to inhibitory gaba subtype receptors, and modulates chloride currents through receptor channels. It also inhibits glutamate induced depolarizations. [NIH]

Potassium: An element that is in the alkali group of metals. It has an atomic symbol K, atomic number 19, and atomic weight 39.10. It is the chief cation in the intracellular fluid of muscle and other cells. Potassium ion is a strong electrolyte and it plays a significant role in the regulation of fluid volume and maintenance of the water-electrolyte balance. [NIH]

Riboflavin: Nutritional factor found in milk, eggs, malted barley, liver, kidney, heart, and leafy vegetables. The richest natural source is yeast. It occurs in the free form only in the retina of the eye, in whey, and in urine; its principal forms in tissues and cells are as FMN and FAD. [NIH]

Selenium: An element with the atomic symbol Se, atomic number 34, and atomic weight 78.96. It is an essential micronutrient for mammals and other animals but is toxic in large amounts. Selenium protects intracellular structures against oxidative damage. It is an essential component of glutathione peroxidase. [NIH]

Thyroxine: An amino acid of the thyroid gland which exerts a stimulating effect on thyroid metabolism. [NIH]

APPENDIX D. FINDING MEDICAL LIBRARIES

Overview

At a medical library you can find medical texts and reference books, consumer health publications, specialty newspapers and magazines, as well as medical journals. In this Appendix, we show you how to quickly find a medical library in your area.

Preparation

Before going to the library, highlight the references mentioned in this sourcebook that you find interesting. Focus on those items that are not available via the Internet, and ask the reference librarian for help with your search. He or she may know of additional resources that could be helpful to you. Most importantly, your local public library and medical libraries have Interlibrary Loan programs with the National Library of Medicine (NLM), one of the largest medical collections in the world. According to the NLM, most of the literature in the general and historical collections of the National Library of Medicine is available on interlibrary loan to any library. NLM's interlibrary loan services are only available to libraries. If you would like to access NLM medical literature, then visit a library in your area that can request the publications for you.[47]

---

[47] Adapted from the NLM: **http://www.nlm.nih.gov/psd/cas/interlibrary.html**

Finding a Local Medical Library

The quickest method to locate medical libraries is to use the Internet-based directory published by the National Network of Libraries of Medicine (NN/LM). This network includes 4626 members and affiliates that provide many services to librarians, health professionals, and the public. To find a library in your area, simply visit **http://nnlm.gov/members/adv.html** or call 1-800-338-7657.

Medical Libraries Open to the Public

In addition to the NN/LM, the National Library of Medicine (NLM) lists a number of libraries that are generally open to the public and have reference facilities. The following is the NLM's list plus hyperlinks to each library Web site. These Web pages can provide information on hours of operation and other restrictions. The list below is a small sample of libraries recommended by the National Library of Medicine (sorted alphabetically by name of the U.S. state or Canadian province where the library is located):[48]

- **Alabama:** Health InfoNet of Jefferson County (Jefferson County Library Cooperative, Lister Hill Library of the Health Sciences), **http://www.uab.edu/infonet/**

- **Alabama:** Richard M. Scrushy Library (American Sports Medicine Institute), **http://www.asmi.org/LIBRARY.HTM**

- **Arizona:** Samaritan Regional Medical Center: The Learning Center (Samaritan Health System, Phoenix, Arizona), **http://www.samaritan.edu/library/bannerlibs.htm**

- **California:** Kris Kelly Health Information Center (St. Joseph Health System), **http://www.humboldt1.com/~kkhic/index.html**

- **California:** Community Health Library of Los Gatos (Community Health Library of Los Gatos), **http://www.healthlib.org/orgresources.html**

- **California:** Consumer Health Program and Services (CHIPS) (County of Los Angeles Public Library, Los Angeles County Harbor-UCLA Medical Center Library) - Carson, CA, **http://www.colapublib.org/services/chips.html**

- **California:** Gateway Health Library (Sutter Gould Medical Foundation)

- **California:** Health Library (Stanford University Medical Center), **http://www-med.stanford.edu/healthlibrary/**

---

[48] Abstracted from **http://www.nlm.nih.gov/medlineplus/libraries.html**

- **California:** Patient Education Resource Center - Health Information and Resources (University of California, San Francisco), **http://sfghdean.ucsf.edu/barnett/PERC/default.asp**

- **California:** Redwood Health Library (Petaluma Health Care District), **http://www.phcd.org/rdwdlib.html**

- **California:** San José PlaneTree Health Library, **http://planetreesanjose.org/**

- **California:** Sutter Resource Library (Sutter Hospitals Foundation), **http://go.sutterhealth.org/comm/resc-library/sac-resources.html**

- **California:** University of California, Davis. Health Sciences Libraries

- **California:** ValleyCare Health Library & Ryan Comer Cancer Resource Center (ValleyCare Health System), **http://www.valleycare.com/library.html**

- **California:** Washington Community Health Resource Library (Washington Community Health Resource Library), **http://www.healthlibrary.org/**

- **Colorado:** William V. Gervasini Memorial Library (Exempla Healthcare), **http://www.exempla.org/conslib.htm**

- **Connecticut:** Hartford Hospital Health Science Libraries (Hartford Hospital), **http://www.harthosp.org/library/**

- **Connecticut:** Healthnet: Connecticut Consumer Health Information Center (University of Connecticut Health Center, Lyman Maynard Stowe Library), **http://library.uchc.edu/departm/hnet/**

- **Connecticut:** Waterbury Hospital Health Center Library (Waterbury Hospital), **http://www.waterburyhospital.com/library/consumer.shtml**

- **Delaware:** Consumer Health Library (Christiana Care Health System, Eugene du Pont Preventive Medicine & Rehabilitation Institute), **http://www.christianacare.org/health_guide/health_guide_pmri_health _info.cfm**

- **Delaware:** Lewis B. Flinn Library (Delaware Academy of Medicine), **http://www.delamed.org/chls.html**

- **Georgia:** Family Resource Library (Medical College of Georgia), **http://cmc.mcg.edu/kids_families/fam_resources/fam_res_lib/frl.htm**

- **Georgia:** Health Resource Center (Medical Center of Central Georgia), **http://www.mccg.org/hrc/hrchome.asp**

- **Hawaii:** Hawaii Medical Library: Consumer Health Information Service (Hawaii Medical Library), **http://hml.org/CHIS/**

- **Idaho:** DeArmond Consumer Health Library (Kootenai Medical Center), http://www.nicon.org/DeArmond/index.htm

- **Illinois:** Health Learning Center of Northwestern Memorial Hospital (Northwestern Memorial Hospital, Health Learning Center), http://www.nmh.org/health_info/hlc.html

- **Illinois:** Medical Library (OSF Saint Francis Medical Center), http://www.osfsaintfrancis.org/general/library/

- **Kentucky:** Medical Library - Services for Patients, Families, Students & the Public (Central Baptist Hospital), http://www.centralbap.com/education/community/library.htm

- **Kentucky:** University of Kentucky - Health Information Library (University of Kentucky, Chandler Medical Center, Health Information Library), http://www.mc.uky.edu/PatientEd/

- **Louisiana:** Alton Ochsner Medical Foundation Library (Alton Ochsner Medical Foundation), http://www.ochsner.org/library/

- **Louisiana:** Louisiana State University Health Sciences Center Medical Library-Shreveport, http://lib-sh.lsuhsc.edu/

- **Maine:** Franklin Memorial Hospital Medical Library (Franklin Memorial Hospital), http://www.fchn.org/fmh/lib.htm

- **Maine:** Gerrish-True Health Sciences Library (Central Maine Medical Center), http://www.cmmc.org/library/library.html

- **Maine:** Hadley Parrot Health Science Library (Eastern Maine Healthcare), http://www.emh.org/hll/hpl/guide.htm

- **Maine:** Maine Medical Center Library (Maine Medical Center), http://www.mmc.org/library/

- **Maine:** Parkview Hospital, http://www.parkviewhospital.org/communit.htm#Library

- **Maine:** Southern Maine Medical Center Health Sciences Library (Southern Maine Medical Center), http://www.smmc.org/services/service.php3?choice=10

- **Maine:** Stephens Memorial Hospital Health Information Library (Western Maine Health), http://www.wmhcc.com/hil_frame.html

- **Manitoba, Canada:** Consumer & Patient Health Information Service (University of Manitoba Libraries), http://www.umanitoba.ca/libraries/units/health/reference/chis.html

- **Manitoba, Canada:** J.W. Crane Memorial Library (Deer Lodge Centre), http://www.deerlodge.mb.ca/library/libraryservices.shtml

- **Maryland:** Health Information Center at the Wheaton Regional Library (Montgomery County, Md., Dept. of Public Libraries, Wheaton Regional Library), **http://www.mont.lib.md.us/healthinfo/hic.asp**

- **Massachusetts:** Baystate Medical Center Library (Baystate Health System), **http://www.baystatehealth.com/1024/**

- **Massachusetts:** Boston University Medical Center Alumni Medical Library (Boston University Medical Center), **http://med-libwww.bu.edu/library/lib.html**

- **Massachusetts:** Lowell General Hospital Health Sciences Library (Lowell General Hospital), **http://www.lowellgeneral.org/library/HomePageLinks/WWW.htm**

- **Massachusetts:** Paul E. Woodard Health Sciences Library (New England Baptist Hospital), **http://www.nebh.org/health_lib.asp**

- **Massachusetts:** St. Luke's Hospital Health Sciences Library (St. Luke's Hospital), **http://www.southcoast.org/library/**

- **Massachusetts:** Treadwell Library Consumer Health Reference Center (Massachusetts General Hospital), **http://www.mgh.harvard.edu/library/chrcindex.html**

- **Massachusetts:** UMass HealthNet (University of Massachusetts Medical School), **http://healthnet.umassmed.edu/**

- **Michigan:** Botsford General Hospital Library - Consumer Health (Botsford General Hospital, Library & Internet Services), **http://www.botsfordlibrary.org/consumer.htm**

- **Michigan:** Helen DeRoy Medical Library (Providence Hospital and Medical Centers), **http://www.providence-hospital.org/library/**

- **Michigan:** Marquette General Hospital - Consumer Health Library (Marquette General Hospital, Health Information Center), **http://www.mgh.org/center.html**

- **Michigan:** Patient Education Resouce Center - University of Michigan Cancer Center (University of Michigan Comprehensive Cancer Center), **http://www.cancer.med.umich.edu/learn/leares.htm**

- **Michigan:** Sladen Library & Center for Health Information Resources - Consumer Health Information, **http://www.sladen.hfhs.org/library/consumer/index.html**

- **Montana:** Center for Health Information (St. Patrick Hospital and Health Sciences Center), **http://www.saintpatrick.org/chi/librarydetail.php3?ID=41**

- **National:** Consumer Health Library Directory (Medical Library Association, Consumer and Patient Health Information Section), **http://caphis.mlanet.org/directory/index.html**

- **National:** National Network of Libraries of Medicine (National Library of Medicine) - provides library services for health professionals in the United States who do not have access to a medical library, **http://nnlm.gov/**

- **National:** NN/LM List of Libraries Serving the Public (National Network of Libraries of Medicine), **http://nnlm.gov/members/**

- **Nevada:** Health Science Library, West Charleston Library (Las Vegas Clark County Library District), **http://www.lvccld.org/special_collections/medical/index.htm**

- **New Hampshire:** Dartmouth Biomedical Libraries (Dartmouth College Library), **http://www.dartmouth.edu/~biomed/resources.htmld/conshealth.htmld/**

- **New Jersey:** Consumer Health Library (Rahway Hospital), **http://www.rahwayhospital.com/library.htm**

- **New Jersey:** Dr. Walter Phillips Health Sciences Library (Englewood Hospital and Medical Center), **http://www.englewoodhospital.com/links/index.htm**

- **New Jersey:** Meland Foundation (Englewood Hospital and Medical Center), **http://www.geocities.com/ResearchTriangle/9360/**

- **New York:** Choices in Health Information (New York Public Library) - NLM Consumer Pilot Project participant, **http://www.nypl.org/branch/health/links.html**

- **New York:** Health Information Center (Upstate Medical University, State University of New York), **http://www.upstate.edu/library/hic/**

- **New York:** Health Sciences Library (Long Island Jewish Medical Center), **http://www.lij.edu/library/library.html**

- **New York:** ViaHealth Medical Library (Rochester General Hospital), **http://www.nyam.org/library/**

- **Ohio:** Consumer Health Library (Akron General Medical Center, Medical & Consumer Health Library), **http://www.akrongeneral.org/hwlibrary.htm**

- **Oklahoma:** Saint Francis Health System Patient/Family Resource Center (Saint Francis Health System), **http://www.sfh-tulsa.com/patientfamilycenter/default.asp**

- **Oregon:** Planetree Health Resource Center (Mid-Columbia Medical Center), **http://www.mcmc.net/phrc/**

- **Pennsylvania:** Community Health Information Library (Milton S. Hershey Medical Center), **http://www.hmc.psu.edu/commhealth/**

- **Pennsylvania:** Community Health Resource Library (Geisinger Medical Center), **http://www.geisinger.edu/education/commlib.shtml**

- **Pennsylvania:** HealthInfo Library (Moses Taylor Hospital), **http://www.mth.org/healthwellness.html**

- **Pennsylvania:** Hopwood Library (University of Pittsburgh, Health Sciences Library System), **http://www.hsls.pitt.edu/chi/hhrcinfo.html**

- **Pennsylvania:** Koop Community Health Information Center (College of Physicians of Philadelphia), **http://www.collphyphil.org/kooppg1.shtml**

- **Pennsylvania:** Learning Resources Center - Medical Library (Susquehanna Health System), **http://www.shscares.org/services/lrc/index.asp**

- **Pennsylvania:** Medical Library (UPMC Health System), **http://www.upmc.edu/passavant/library.htm**

- **Quebec, Canada:** Medical Library (Montreal General Hospital), **http://ww2.mcgill.ca/mghlib/**

- **South Dakota:** Rapid City Regional Hospital - Health Information Center (Rapid City Regional Hospital, Health Information Center), **http://www.rcrh.org/education/LibraryResourcesConsumers.htm**

- **Texas:** Houston HealthWays (Houston Academy of Medicine-Texas Medical Center Library), **http://hhw.library.tmc.edu/**

- **Texas:** Matustik Family Resource Center (Cook Children's Health Care System), **http://www.cookchildrens.com/Matustik_Library.html**

- **Washington:** Community Health Library (Kittitas Valley Community Hospital), **http://www.kvch.com/**

- **Washington:** Southwest Washington Medical Center Library (Southwest Washington Medical Center), **http://www.swmedctr.com/Home/**

APPENDIX E. YOUR RIGHTS AND INSURANCE

Overview

Any patient with apraxia faces a series of issues related more to the healthcare industry than to the medical condition itself. This appendix covers two important topics in this regard: your rights and responsibilities as a patient, and how to get the most out of your medical insurance plan.

Your Rights as a Patient

The President's Advisory Commission on Consumer Protection and Quality in the Healthcare Industry has created the following summary of your rights as a patient.[49]

Information Disclosure

Consumers have the right to receive accurate, easily understood information. Some consumers require assistance in making informed decisions about health plans, health professionals, and healthcare facilities. Such information includes:

- *Health plans.* Covered benefits, cost-sharing, and procedures for resolving complaints, licensure, certification, and accreditation status, comparable measures of quality and consumer satisfaction, provider network composition, the procedures that govern access to specialists and emergency services, and care management information.

---

[49]Adapted from Consumer Bill of Rights and Responsibilities:
http://www.hcqualitycommission.gov/press/cbor.html#head1.

- *Health professionals.* Education, board certification, and recertification, years of practice, experience performing certain procedures, and comparable measures of quality and consumer satisfaction.

- *Healthcare facilities.* Experience in performing certain procedures and services, accreditation status, comparable measures of quality, worker, and consumer satisfaction, and procedures for resolving complaints.

- *Consumer assistance programs.* Programs must be carefully structured to promote consumer confidence and to work cooperatively with health plans, providers, payers, and regulators. Desirable characteristics of such programs are sponsorship that ensures accountability to the interests of consumers and stable, adequate funding.

Choice of Providers and Plans

Consumers have the right to a choice of healthcare providers that is sufficient to ensure access to appropriate high-quality healthcare. To ensure such choice, the Commission recommends the following:

- *Provider network adequacy.* All health plan networks should provide access to sufficient numbers and types of providers to assure that all covered services will be accessible without unreasonable delay -- including access to emergency services 24 hours a day and 7 days a week. If a health plan has an insufficient number or type of providers to provide a covered benefit with the appropriate degree of specialization, the plan should ensure that the consumer obtains the benefit outside the network at no greater cost than if the benefit were obtained from participating providers.

- *Women's health services.* Women should be able to choose a qualified provider offered by a plan -- such as gynecologists, certified nurse midwives, and other qualified healthcare providers -- for the provision of covered care necessary to provide routine and preventative women's healthcare services.

- *Access to specialists.* Consumers with complex or serious medical conditions who require frequent specialty care should have direct access to a qualified specialist of their choice within a plan's network of providers. Authorizations, when required, should be for an adequate number of direct access visits under an approved treatment plan.

- *Transitional care.* Consumers who are undergoing a course of treatment for a chronic or disabling condition (or who are in the second or third trimester of a pregnancy) at the time they involuntarily change health plans or at a time when a provider is terminated by a plan for other than cause should be able to continue seeing their current specialty providers for up to 90 days (or through completion of postpartum care) to allow for transition of care.

- *Choice of health plans.* Public and private group purchasers should, wherever feasible, offer consumers a choice of high-quality health insurance plans.

Access to Emergency Services

Consumers have the right to access emergency healthcare services when and where the need arises. Health plans should provide payment when a consumer presents to an emergency department with acute symptoms of sufficient severity--including severe pain--such that a "prudent layperson" could reasonably expect the absence of medical attention to result in placing that consumer's health in serious jeopardy, serious impairment to bodily functions, or serious dysfunction of any bodily organ or part.

Participation in Treatment Decisions

Consumers have the right and responsibility to fully participate in all decisions related to their healthcare. Consumers who are unable to fully participate in treatment decisions have the right to be represented by parents, guardians, family members, or other conservators. Physicians and other health professionals should:

- Provide patients with sufficient information and opportunity to decide among treatment options consistent with the informed consent process.

- Discuss all treatment options with a patient in a culturally competent manner, including the option of no treatment at all.

- Ensure that persons with disabilities have effective communications with members of the health system in making such decisions.

- Discuss all current treatments a consumer may be undergoing.

- Discuss all risks, benefits, and consequences to treatment or nontreatment.

- Give patients the opportunity to refuse treatment and to express preferences about future treatment decisions.

- Discuss the use of advance directives -- both living wills and durable powers of attorney for healthcare -- with patients and their designated family members.

- Abide by the decisions made by their patients and/or their designated representatives consistent with the informed consent process.

Health plans, health providers, and healthcare facilities should:

- Disclose to consumers factors -- such as methods of compensation, ownership of or interest in healthcare facilities, or matters of conscience -- that could influence advice or treatment decisions.

- Assure that provider contracts do not contain any so-called "gag clauses" or other contractual mechanisms that restrict healthcare providers' ability to communicate with and advise patients about medically necessary treatment options.

- Be prohibited from penalizing or seeking retribution against healthcare professionals or other health workers for advocating on behalf of their patients.

Respect and Nondiscrimination

Consumers have the right to considerate, respectful care from all members of the healthcare industry at all times and under all circumstances. An environment of mutual respect is essential to maintain a quality healthcare system. To assure that right, the Commission recommends the following:

- Consumers must not be discriminated against in the delivery of healthcare services consistent with the benefits covered in their policy, or as required by law, based on race, ethnicity, national origin, religion, sex, age, mental or physical disability, sexual orientation, genetic information, or source of payment.

- Consumers eligible for coverage under the terms and conditions of a health plan or program, or as required by law, must not be discriminated against in marketing and enrollment practices based on race, ethnicity, national origin, religion, sex, age, mental or physical disability, sexual orientation, genetic information, or source of payment.

Confidentiality of Health Information

Consumers have the right to communicate with healthcare providers in confidence and to have the confidentiality of their individually identifiable healthcare information protected. Consumers also have the right to review and copy their own medical records and request amendments to their records.

Complaints and Appeals

Consumers have the right to a fair and efficient process for resolving differences with their health plans, healthcare providers, and the institutions that serve them, including a rigorous system of internal review and an independent system of external review. A free copy of the Patient's Bill of Rights is available from the American Hospital Association.[50]

Patient Responsibilities

Treatment is a two-way street between you and your healthcare providers. To underscore the importance of finance in modern healthcare as well as your responsibility for the financial aspects of your care, the President's Advisory Commission on Consumer Protection and Quality in the Healthcare Industry has proposed that patients understand the following "Consumer Responsibilities."[51] In a healthcare system that protects consumers' rights, it is reasonable to expect and encourage consumers to assume certain responsibilities. Greater individual involvement by the consumer in his or her care increases the likelihood of achieving the best outcome and helps support a quality-oriented, cost-conscious environment. Such responsibilities include:

- Take responsibility for maximizing healthy habits such as exercising, not smoking, and eating a healthy diet.

- Work collaboratively with healthcare providers in developing and carrying out agreed-upon treatment plans.

- Disclose relevant information and clearly communicate wants and needs.

- Use your health insurance plan's internal complaint and appeal processes to address your concerns.

- Avoid knowingly spreading disease.

---

[50] To order your free copy of the Patient's Bill of Rights, telephone 312-422-3000 or visit the American Hospital Association's Web site: **http://www.aha.org**. Click on "Resource Center," go to "Search" at bottom of page, and then type in "Patient's Bill of Rights." The Patient's Bill of Rights is also available from Fax on Demand, at 312-422-2020, document number 471124.

[51] Adapted from **http://www.hcqualitycommission.gov/press/cbor.html#head1**.

- Recognize the reality of risks, the limits of the medical science, and the human fallibility of the healthcare professional.

- Be aware of a healthcare provider's obligation to be reasonably efficient and equitable in providing care to other patients and the community.

- Become knowledgeable about your health plan's coverage and options (when available) including all covered benefits, limitations, and exclusions, rules regarding use of network providers, coverage and referral rules, appropriate processes to secure additional information, and the process to appeal coverage decisions.

- Show respect for other patients and health workers.

- Make a good-faith effort to meet financial obligations.

- Abide by administrative and operational procedures of health plans, healthcare providers, and Government health benefit programs.

Choosing an Insurance Plan

There are a number of official government agencies that help consumers understand their healthcare insurance choices.[52] The U.S. Department of Labor, in particular, recommends ten ways to make your health benefits choices work best for you.[53]

1. Your options are important. There are many different types of health benefit plans. Find out which one your employer offers, then check out the plan, or plans, offered. Your employer's human resource office, the health plan administrator, or your union can provide information to help you match your needs and preferences with the available plans. The more information you have, the better your healthcare decisions will be.

2. Reviewing the benefits available. Do the plans offered cover preventive care, well-baby care, vision or dental care? Are there deductibles? Answers to these questions can help determine the out-of-pocket expenses you may face. Matching your needs and those of your family members will result in the best possible benefits. Cheapest may not always be best. Your goal is high quality health benefits.

---

[52] More information about quality across programs is provided at the following AHRQ Web site:
http://www.ahrq.gov/consumer/qntascii/qnthplan.htm.
[53] Adapted from the Department of Labor:
http://www.dol.gov/dol/pwba/public/pubs/health/top10-text.html.

3. Look for quality. The quality of healthcare services varies, but quality can be measured. You should consider the quality of healthcare in deciding among the healthcare plans or options available to you. Not all health plans, doctors, hospitals and other providers give the highest quality care. Fortunately, there is quality information you can use right now to help you compare your healthcare choices. Find out how you can measure quality. Consult the U.S. Department of Health and Human Services publication "Your Guide to Choosing Quality Health Care" on the Internet at **www.ahcpr.gov/consumer.**

4. Your plan's summary plan description (SPD) provides a wealth of information. Your health plan administrator can provide you with a copy of your plan's SPD. It outlines your benefits and your legal rights under the Employee Retirement Income Security Act (ERISA), the federal law that protects your health benefits. It should contain information about the coverage of dependents, what services will require a co-pay, and the circumstances under which your employer can change or terminate a health benefits plan. Save the SPD and all other health plan brochures and documents, along with memos or correspondence from your employer relating to health benefits.

5. Assess your benefit coverage as your family status changes. Marriage, divorce, childbirth or adoption, and the death of a spouse are all life events that may signal a need to change your health benefits. You, your spouse and dependent children may be eligible for a special enrollment period under provisions of the Health Insurance Portability and Accountability Act (HIPAA). Even without life-changing events, the information provided by your employer should tell you how you can change benefits or switch plans, if more than one plan is offered. If your spouse's employer also offers a health benefits package, consider coordinating both plans for maximum coverage.

6. Changing jobs and other life events can affect your health benefits. Under the Consolidated Omnibus Budget Reconciliation Act (COBRA), you, your covered spouse, and your dependent children may be eligible to purchase extended health coverage under your employer's plan if you lose your job, change employers, get divorced, or upon occurrence of certain other events. Coverage can range from 18 to 36 months depending on your situation. COBRA applies to most employers with 20 or more workers and requires your plan to notify you of your rights. Most plans require eligible individuals to make their COBRA election within 60 days of the plan's notice. Be sure to follow up with your plan sponsor if you don't receive notice, and make sure you respond within the allotted time.

7. HIPAA can also help if you are changing jobs, particularly if you have a medical condition. HIPAA generally limits pre-existing condition exclusions to a maximum of 12 months (18 months for late enrollees). HIPAA also requires this maximum period to be reduced by the length of time you had prior "creditable coverage." You should receive a certificate documenting your prior creditable coverage from your old plan when coverage ends.

8. Plan for retirement. Before you retire, find out what health benefits, if any, extend to you and your spouse during your retirement years. Consult with your employer's human resources office, your union, the plan administrator, and check your SPD. Make sure there is no conflicting information among these sources about the benefits you will receive or the circumstances under which they can change or be eliminated. With this information in hand, you can make other important choices, like finding out if you are eligible for Medicare and Medigap insurance coverage.

9. Know how to file an appeal if your health benefits claim is denied. Understand how your plan handles grievances and where to make appeals of the plan's decisions. Keep records and copies of correspondence. Check your health benefits package and your SPD to determine who is responsible for handling problems with benefit claims. Contact PWBA for customer service assistance if you are unable to obtain a response to your complaint.

10. You can take steps to improve the quality of the healthcare and the health benefits you receive. Look for and use things like Quality Reports and Accreditation Reports whenever you can. Quality reports may contain consumer ratings -- how satisfied consumers are with the doctors in their plan, for instance-- and clinical performance measures -- how well a healthcare organization prevents and treats illness. Accreditation reports provide information on how accredited organizations meet national standards, and often include clinical performance measures. Look for these quality measures whenever possible. Consult "Your Guide to Choosing Quality Health Care" on the Internet at **www.ahcpr.gov/consumer**.

Medicare and Medicaid

Illness strikes both rich and poor families. For low-income families, Medicaid is available to defer the costs of treatment. The Health Care Financing Administration (HCFA) administers Medicare, the nation's largest health insurance program, which covers 39 million Americans. In the following pages, you will learn the basics about Medicare insurance as well as useful contact information on how to find more in-depth information about Medicaid.[54]

Who is Eligible for Medicare?

Generally, you are eligible for Medicare if you or your spouse worked for at least 10 years in Medicare-covered employment and you are 65 years old and a citizen or permanent resident of the United States. You might also qualify for coverage if you are under age 65 but have a disability or End-Stage Renal disease (permanent kidney failure requiring dialysis or transplant). Here are some simple guidelines:

You can get Part A at age 65 without having to pay premiums if:

- You are already receiving retirement benefits from Social Security or the Railroad Retirement Board.

- You are eligible to receive Social Security or Railroad benefits but have not yet filed for them.

- You or your spouse had Medicare-covered government employment.

If you are under 65, you can get Part A without having to pay premiums if:

- You have received Social Security or Railroad Retirement Board disability benefit for 24 months.

- You are a kidney dialysis or kidney transplant patient.

Medicare has two parts:

- Part A (Hospital Insurance). Most people do not have to pay for Part A.

- Part B (Medical Insurance). Most people pay monthly for Part B.

Part A (Hospital Insurance)

Helps Pay For: Inpatient hospital care, care in critical access hospitals (small facilities that give limited outpatient and inpatient services to people in rural areas) and skilled nursing facilities, hospice care, and some home healthcare.

---

[54] This section has been adapted from the Official U.S. Site for Medicare Information: **http://www.medicare.gov/Basics/Overview.asp**.

Cost: Most people get Part A automatically when they turn age 65. You do not have to pay a monthly payment called a premium for Part A because you or a spouse paid Medicare taxes while you were working.

If you (or your spouse) did not pay Medicare taxes while you were working and you are age 65 or older, you still may be able to buy Part A. If you are not sure you have Part A, look on your red, white, and blue Medicare card. It will show "Hospital Part A" on the lower left corner of the card. You can also call the Social Security Administration toll free at 1-800-772-1213 or call your local Social Security office for more information about buying Part A. If you get benefits from the Railroad Retirement Board, call your local RRB office or 1-800-808-0772. For more information, call your Fiscal Intermediary about Part A bills and services. The phone number for the Fiscal Intermediary office in your area can be obtained from the following Web site: **http://www.medicare.gov/Contacts/home.asp**.

Part B (Medical Insurance)

Helps Pay For: Doctors, services, outpatient hospital care, and some other medical services that Part A does not cover, such as the services of physical and occupational therapists, and some home healthcare. Part B helps pay for covered services and supplies when they are medically necessary.

Cost: As of 2001, you pay the Medicare Part B premium of $50.00 per month. In some cases this amount may be higher if you did not choose Part B when you first became eligible at age 65. The cost of Part B may go up 10% for each 12-month period that you were eligible for Part B but declined coverage, except in special cases. You will have to pay the extra 10% cost for the rest of your life.

Enrolling in Part B is your choice. You can sign up for Part B anytime during a 7-month period that begins 3 months before you turn 65. Visit your local Social Security office, or call the Social Security Administration at 1-800-772-1213 to sign up. If you choose to enroll in Part B, the premium is usually taken out of your monthly Social Security, Railroad Retirement, or Civil Service Retirement payment. If you do not receive any of the above payments, Medicare sends you a bill for your part B premium every 3 months. You should receive your Medicare premium bill in the mail by the 10th of the month. If you do not, call the Social Security Administration at 1-800-772-1213, or your local Social Security office. If you get benefits from the Railroad Retirement Board, call your local RRB office or 1-800-808-0772. For more information, call your Medicare carrier about bills and services. The phone number for the Medicare carrier in your area can be found at the following Web site: **http://www.medicare.gov/Contacts/home.asp**. You may have choices in how you get your healthcare including the Original Medicare Plan, Medicare Managed Care Plans (like HMOs), and Medicare Private Fee-for-Service Plans.

Medicaid

Medicaid is a joint federal and state program that helps pay medical costs for some people with low incomes and limited resources. Medicaid programs vary from state to state. People on Medicaid may also get coverage for nursing home care and outpatient prescription drugs which are not covered by Medicare. You can find more information about Medicaid on the HCFA.gov Web site at **http://www.hcfa.gov/medicaid/medicaid.htm**.

States also have programs that pay some or all of Medicare's premiums and may also pay Medicare deductibles and coinsurance for certain people who have Medicare and a low income. To qualify, you must have:

- Part A (Hospital Insurance),

- Assets, such as bank accounts, stocks, and bonds that are not more than $4,000 for a single person, or $6,000 for a couple, and

- A monthly income that is below certain limits.

For more information on these programs, look at the Medicare Savings Programs brochure, **http://www.medicare.gov/Library/PDFNavigation/PDFInterim.asp?Langua ge=English&Type=Pub&PubID=10126**. There are also Prescription Drug Assistance Programs available. Find information on these programs which offer discounts or free medications to individuals in need at **http://www.medicare.gov/Prescription/Home.asp**.

NORD's Medication Assistance Programs

Finally, the National Organization for Rare Disorders, Inc. (NORD) administers medication programs sponsored by humanitarian-minded pharmaceutical and biotechnology companies to help uninsured or under-insured individuals secure life-saving or life-sustaining drugs.[55] NORD

---

[55] Adapted from NORD: **http://www.rarediseases.org/cgi-bin/nord/progserv#patient?id=rPIzL9oD&mv_pc=30**.

programs ensure that certain vital drugs are available "to those individuals whose income is too high to qualify for Medicaid but too low to pay for their prescribed medications." The program has standards for fairness, equity, and unbiased eligibility. It currently covers some 14 programs for nine pharmaceutical companies. NORD also offers early access programs for investigational new drugs (IND) under the approved "Treatment INDs" programs of the Food and Drug Administration (FDA). In these programs, a limited number of individuals can receive investigational drugs that have yet to be approved by the FDA. These programs are generally designed for rare diseases or disorders. For more information, visit **www.rarediseases.org**.

Additional Resources

In addition to the references already listed in this chapter, you may need more information on health insurance, hospitals, or the healthcare system in general. The NIH has set up an excellent guidance Web site that addresses these and other issues. Topics include:[56]

- Health Insurance:
  http://www.nlm.nih.gov/medlineplus/healthinsurance.html

- Health Statistics:
  http://www.nlm.nih.gov/medlineplus/healthstatistics.html

- HMO and Managed Care:
  http://www.nlm.nih.gov/medlineplus/managedcare.html

- Hospice Care: **http://www.nlm.nih.gov/medlineplus/hospicecare.html**

- Medicaid: **http://www.nlm.nih.gov/medlineplus/medicaid.html**

- Medicare: **http://www.nlm.nih.gov/medlineplus/medicare.html**

- Nursing Homes and Long-term Care:
  http://www.nlm.nih.gov/medlineplus/nursinghomes.html

- Patient's Rights, Confidentiality, Informed Consent, Ombudsman Programs, Privacy and Patient Issues:
  http://www.nlm.nih.gov/medlineplus/patientissues.html

---

[56] You can access this information at:
http://www.nlm.nih.gov/medlineplus/healthsystem.html.

ONLINE GLOSSARIES

The Internet provides access to a number of free-to-use medical dictionaries and glossaries. The National Library of Medicine has compiled the following list of online dictionaries:

- ADAM Medical Encyclopedia (A.D.A.M., Inc.), comprehensive medical reference: **http://www.nlm.nih.gov/medlineplus/encyclopedia.html**

- MedicineNet.com Medical Dictionary (MedicineNet, Inc.): **http://www.medterms.com/Script/Main/hp.asp**

- Merriam-Webster Medical Dictionary (Inteli-Health, Inc.): **http://www.intelihealth.com/IH/**

- Multilingual Glossary of Technical and Popular Medical Terms in Eight European Languages (European Commission) - Danish, Dutch, English, French, German, Italian, Portuguese, and Spanish: **http://allserv.rug.ac.be/~rvdstich/eugloss/welcome.html**

- On-line Medical Dictionary (CancerWEB): **http://www.graylab.ac.uk/omd/**

- Technology Glossary (National Library of Medicine) - Health Care Technology: **http://www.nlm.nih.gov/nichsr/ta101/ta10108.htm**

- Terms and Definitions (Office of Rare Diseases): **http://rarediseases.info.nih.gov/ord/glossary_a-e.html**

Beyond these, MEDLINEplus contains a very user-friendly encyclopedia covering every aspect of medicine (licensed from A.D.A.M., Inc.). The ADAM Medical Encyclopedia Web site address is **http://www.nlm.nih.gov/medlineplus/encyclopedia.html**. ADAM is also available on commercial Web sites such as drkoop.com (**http://www.drkoop.com/**) and Web MD (**http://my.webmd.com/adam/asset/adam_disease_articles/a_to_z/a**). Topics of interest can be researched by using keywords before continuing elsewhere, as these basic definitions and concepts will be useful in more advanced areas of research. You may choose to print various pages specifically relating to apraxia and keep them on file.

Online Dictionary Directories

The following are additional online directories compiled by the National Library of Medicine, including a number of specialized medical dictionaries and glossaries:

- Medical Dictionaries: Medical & Biological (World Health Organization): **http://www.who.int/hlt/virtuallibrary/English/diction.htm#Medical**

- MEL-Michigan Electronic Library List of Online Health and Medical Dictionaries (Michigan Electronic Library): **http://mel.lib.mi.us/health/health-dictionaries.html**

- Patient Education: Glossaries (DMOZ Open Directory Project): **http://dmoz.org/Health/Education/Patient_Education/Glossaries/**

- Web of Online Dictionaries (Bucknell University): **http://www.yourdictionary.com/diction5.html#medicine**

APRAXIA GLOSSARY

The following is a complete glossary of terms used in this sourcebook. The definitions are derived from official public sources including the National Institutes of Health [NIH] and the European Union [EU]. After this glossary, we list a number of additional hardbound and electronic glossaries and dictionaries that you may wish to consult.

Agnosia: Loss of the ability to comprehend the meaning or recognize the importance of various forms of stimulation that cannot be attributed to impairment of a primary sensory modality. Tactile agnosia is characterized by an inability to perceive the shape and nature of an object by touch alone, despite unimpaired sensation to light touch, position, and other primary sensory modalities. [NIH]

Amnesia: Lack or loss of memory; inability to remember past experiences. [EU]

Anatomical: Pertaining to anatomy, or to the structure of the organism. [EU]

Anxiety: The unpleasant emotional state consisting of psychophysiological responses to anticipation of unreal or imagined danger, ostensibly resulting from unrecognized intrapsychic conflict. Physiological concomitants include increased heart rate, altered respiration rate, sweating, trembling, weakness, and fatigue; psychological concomitants include feelings of impending danger, powerlessness, apprehension, and tension. [EU]

Aphasia: Defect or loss of the power of expression by speech, writing, or signs, or of comprehending spoken or written language, due to injury or disease of the brain centres. [EU]

Apomorphine: A derivative of morphine that is a dopamine D2 agonist. It is a powerful emetic and has been used for that effect in acute poisoning. It has also been used in the diagnosis and treatment of parkinsonism, but its adverse effects limit its use. [NIH]

Ataxia: Failure of muscular coordination; irregularity of muscular action. [EU]

Atrophy: A wasting away; a diminution in the size of a cell, tissue, organ, or part. [EU]

Atypical: Irregular; not conformable to the type; in microbiology, applied specifically to strains of unusual type. [EU]

Auditory: Pertaining to the sense of hearing. [EU]

Bacteria: Unicellular prokaryotic microorganisms which generally possess rigid cell walls, multiply by cell division, and exhibit three principal forms:

round or coccal, rodlike or bacillary, and spiral or spirochetal. [NIH]

Bilateral: Having two sides, or pertaining to both sides. [EU]

Blepharitis: Inflammation of the eyelids. [EU]

Blepharospasm: Excessive winking; tonic or clonic spasm of the orbicularis oculi muscle. [NIH]

Blinking: Brief closing of the eyelids by involuntary normal periodic closing, as a protective measure, or by voluntary action. [NIH]

Capsules: Hard or soft soluble containers used for the oral administration of medicine. [NIH]

Carbohydrate: An aldehyde or ketone derivative of a polyhydric alcohol, particularly of the pentahydric and hexahydric alcohols. They are so named because the hydrogen and oxygen are usually in the proportion to form water, $(CH_2O)n$. The most important carbohydrates are the starches, sugars, celluloses, and gums. They are classified into mono-, di-, tri-, poly- and heterosaccharides. [EU]

Cerebellum: Part of the metencephalon that lies in the posterior cranial fossa behind the brain stem. It is concerned with the coordination of movement. [NIH]

Cerebral: Of or pertaining of the cerebrum or the brain. [EU]

Cholesterol: The principal sterol of all higher animals, distributed in body tissues, especially the brain and spinal cord, and in animal fats and oils. [NIH]

Cognition: Intellectual or mental process whereby an organism becomes aware of or obtains knowledge. [NIH]

Colic: Paroxysms of pain. This condition usually occurs in the abdominal region but may occur in other body regions as well. [NIH]

Concomitant: Accompanying; accessory; joined with another. [EU]

Confusion: Disturbed orientation in regard to time, place, or person, sometimes accompanied by disordered consciousness. [EU]

Cornea: The transparent structure forming the anterior part of the fibrous tunic of the eye. It consists of five layers : (1) the anterior corneal epithelium, continuous with that of the conjunctiva, (2) the anterior limiting layer (Bowman's membrane), (3) the substantia propria, or stroma, (4) the posterior limiting layer (Descemet's membrane), and (5) the endothelium of the anterior chamber, called also keratoderma. [EU]

Cortex: The outer layer of an organ or other body structure, as distinguished from the internal substance. [EU]

Cortical: Pertaining to or of the nature of a cortex or bark. [EU]

Cues: Signals for an action; that specific portion of a perceptual field or pattern of stimuli to which a subject has learned to respond. [NIH]

Dementia: An acquired organic mental disorder with loss of intellectual abilities of sufficient severity to interfere with social or occupational functioning. The dysfunction is multifaceted and involves memory, behavior, personality, judgment, attention, spatial relations, language, abstract thought, and other executive functions. The intellectual decline is usually progressive, and initially spares the level of consciousness. [NIH]

Diarrhea: Passage of excessively liquid or excessively frequent stools. [NIH]

Distal: Remote; farther from any point of reference; opposed to proximal. In dentistry, used to designate a position on the dental arch farther from the median line of the jaw. [EU]

Dizziness: An imprecise term which may refer to a sense of spatial disorientation, motion of the environment, or lightheadedness. [NIH]

Dorsal: 1. pertaining to the back or to any dorsum. 2. denoting a position more toward the back surface than some other object of reference; same as posterior in human anatomy; superior in the anatomy of quadrupeds. [EU]

Dysarthria: Imperfect articulation of speech due to disturbances of muscular control which result from damage to the central or peripheral nervous system. [EU]

Dyskinesia: Impairment of the power of voluntary movement, resulting in fragmentary or incomplete movements. [EU]

Dysphagia: Difficulty in swallowing. [EU]

Elective: Subject to the choice or decision of the patient or physician; applied to procedures that are advantageous to the patient but not urgent. [EU]

Electroencephalography: The recording of the electric currents developed in the brain, by means of electrodes applied to the scalp, to the surface of the brain (intracranial e.) or placed within the substance of the brain (depth e.). [EU]

Electromyography: Recording of the changes in electric potential of muscle by means of surface or needle electrodes. [NIH]

Enzyme: A protein molecule that catalyses chemical reactions of other substances without itself being destroyed or altered upon completion of the reactions. Enzymes are classified according to the recommendations of the Nomenclature Committee of the International Union of Biochemistry. Each enzyme is assigned a recommended name and an Enzyme Commission (EC) number. They are divided into six main groups; oxidoreductases, transferases, hydrolases, lyases, isomerases, and ligases. [EU]

Flaccid: Weak, lax and soft. [EU]

Gait: Manner or style of walking. [NIH]

Genotype: The genetic constitution of the individual; the characterization of the genes. [NIH]

Gestures: Movement of a part of the body for the purpose of communication. [NIH]

Histidine: An essential amino acid important in a number of metabolic processes. It is required for the production of histamine. [NIH]

Hydrocephalus: A condition marked by dilatation of the cerebral ventricles, most often occurring secondarily to obstruction of the cerebrospinal fluid pathways, and accompanied by an accumulation of cerebrospinal fluid within the skull; the fluid is usually under increased pressure, but occasionally may be normal or nearly so. It is typically characterized by enlargement of the head, prominence of the forehead, brain atrophy, mental deterioration, and convulsions; may be congenital or acquired; and may be of sudden onset (acute h.) or be slowly progressive (chronic or primary h.). [EU]

Hypotonia: A condition of diminished tone of the skeletal muscles; diminished resistance of muscles to passive stretching. [EU]

Idiopathic: Of the nature of an idiopathy; self-originated; of unknown causation. [EU]

Inflammation: A pathological process characterized by injury or destruction of tissues caused by a variety of cytologic and chemical reactions. It is usually manifested by typical signs of pain, heat, redness, swelling, and loss of function. [NIH]

Intestinal: Pertaining to the intestine. [EU]

Iodine: A nonmetallic element of the halogen group that is represented by the atomic symbol I, atomic number 53, and atomic weight of 126.90. It is a nutritionally essential element, especially important in thyroid hormone synthesis. In solution, it has anti-infective properties and is used topically. [NIH]

Keratitis: Inflammation of the cornea. [EU]

Kinetic: Pertaining to or producing motion. [EU]

Laryngectomy: Total or partial excision of the larynx. [NIH]

Larynx: An irregularly shaped, musculocartilaginous tubular structure, lined with mucous membrane, located at the top of the trachea and below the root of the tongue and the hyoid bone. It is the essential sphincter guarding the entrance into the trachea and functioning secondarily as the organ of voice. [NIH]

Lesion: Any pathological or traumatic discontinuity of tissue or loss of function of a part. [EU]

Lethal: Deadly, fatal. [EU]

Levodopa: The naturally occurring form of dopa and the immediate precursor of dopamine. Unlike dopamine itself, it can be taken orally and crosses the blood-brain barrier. It is rapidly taken up by dopaminergic neurons and converted to dopamine. It is used for the treatment of parkinsonism and is usually given with agents that inhibit its conversion to dopamine outside of the central nervous system. [NIH]

Lip: Either of the two fleshy, full-blooded margins of the mouth. [NIH]

Lobe: A more or less well-defined portion of any organ, especially of the brain, lungs, and glands. Lobes are demarcated by fissures, sulci, connective tissue, and by their shape. [EU]

Localization: 1. the determination of the site or place of any process or lesion. 2. restriction to a circumscribed or limited area. 3. prelocalization. [EU]

Microbiology: The study of microorganisms such as fungi, bacteria, algae, archaea, and viruses. [NIH]

Molecular: Of, pertaining to, or composed of molecules : a very small mass of matter. [EU]

Musculature: The muscular apparatus of the body, or of any part of it. [EU]

Mutism: Inability or refusal to speak. [EU]

Neural: 1. pertaining to a nerve or to the nerves. 2. situated in the region of the spinal axis, as the neutral arch. [EU]

Neuroanatomy: Study of the anatomy of the nervous system as a specialty or discipline. [NIH]

Neurology: A medical specialty concerned with the study of the structures, functions, and diseases of the nervous system. [NIH]

Neurons: The basic cellular units of nervous tissue. Each neuron consists of a body, an axon, and dendrites. Their purpose is to receive, conduct, and transmit impulses in the nervous system. [NIH]

Neurophysiology: The scientific discipline concerned with the physiology of the nervous system. [NIH]

Neuropsychology: A branch of psychology which investigates the correlation between experience or behavior and the basic neurophysiological processes. The term neuropsychology stresses the dominant role of the nervous system. It is a more narrowly defined field than physiological psychology or psychophysiology. [NIH]

Neurosurgery: A surgical specialty concerned with the treatment of diseases and disorders of the brain, spinal cord, and peripheral and sympathetic nervous system. [NIH]

Niacin: Water-soluble vitamin of the B complex occurring in various animal and plant tissues. Required by the body for the formation of coenzymes

NAD and NADP. Has pellagra-curative, vasodilating, and antilipemic properties. [NIH]

Ocular: 1. of, pertaining to, or affecting the eye. 2. eyepiece. [EU]

Oral: Pertaining to the mouth, taken through or applied in the mouth, as an oral medication or an oral thermometer. [EU]

Ototoxic: Having a deleterious effect upon the eighth nerve, or upon the organs of hearing and balance. [EU]

Overdose: 1. to administer an excessive dose. 2. an excessive dose. [EU]

Parietal: 1. of or pertaining to the walls of a cavity. 2. pertaining to or located near the parietal bone, as the parietal lobe. [EU]

Parkinsonism: A group of neurological disorders characterized by hypokinesia, tremor, and muscular rigidity. [EU]

Pediatrics: A medical specialty concerned with maintaining health and providing medical care to children from birth to adolescence. [NIH]

Phenobarbital: A barbituric acid derivative that acts as a nonselective central nervous system depressant. It promotes binding to inhibitory gaba subtype receptors, and modulates chloride currents through receptor channels. It also inhibits glutamate induced depolarizations. [NIH]

Phenotype: The outward appearance of the individual. It is the product of interactions between genes and between the genotype and the environment. This includes the killer phenotype, characteristic of yeasts. [NIH]

Phobia: A persistent, irrational, intense fear of a specific object, activity, or situation (the phobic stimulus), fear that is recognized as being excessive or unreasonable by the individual himself. When a phobia is a significant source of distress or interferes with social functioning, it is considered a mental disorder; phobic disorder (or neurosis). In DSM III phobic disorders are subclassified as agoraphobia, social phobias, and simple phobias. Used as a word termination denoting irrational fear of or aversion to the subject indicated by the stem to which it is affixed. [EU]

Phonation: The process of producing vocal sounds by means of vocal cords vibrating in an expiratory blast of air. [NIH]

Photophobia: Abnormal visual intolerance of light. [EU]

Polypeptide: A peptide which on hydrolysis yields more than two amino acids; called tripeptides, tetrapeptides, etc. according to the number of amino acids contained. [EU]

Polyphosphates: Linear polymers in which orthophosphate residues are linked with energy-rich phosphoanhydride bonds. They are found in plants, animals, and microorganisms. [NIH]

Posterior: Situated in back of, or in the back part of, or affecting the back or dorsal surface of the body. In lower animals, it refers to the caudal end of the body. [EU]

Potassium: An element that is in the alkali group of metals. It has an atomic symbol K, atomic number 19, and atomic weight 39.10. It is the chief cation in the intracellular fluid of muscle and other cells. Potassium ion is a strong electrolyte and it plays a significant role in the regulation of fluid volume and maintenance of the water-electrolyte balance. [NIH]

Prejudice: A preconceived judgment made without adequate evidence and not easily alterable by presentation of contrary evidence. [NIH]

Prevalence: The total number of cases of a given disease in a specified population at a designated time. It is differentiated from incidence, which refers to the number of new cases in the population at a given time. [NIH]

Progressive: Advancing; going forward; going from bad to worse; increasing in scope or severity. [EU]

Proteins: Polymers of amino acids linked by peptide bonds. The specific sequence of amino acids determines the shape and function of the protein. [NIH]

Proximal: Nearest; closer to any point of reference; opposed to distal. [EU]

Psychiatric: Pertaining to or within the purview of psychiatry. [EU]

Psychiatry: The medical science that deals with the origin, diagnosis, prevention, and treatment of mental disorders. [NIH]

Psychology: The science dealing with the study of mental processes and behavior in man and animals. [NIH]

Psychosomatic: Pertaining to the mind-body relationship; having bodily symptoms of psychic, emotional, or mental origin; called also psychophysiologic. [EU]

Psychotherapy: A generic term for the treatment of mental illness or emotional disturbances primarily by verbal or nonverbal communication. [NIH]

Retraction: 1. the act of drawing back; the condition of being drawn back. 2. distal movement of teeth, usually accomplished with an orthodontic appliance. [EU]

Riboflavin: Nutritional factor found in milk, eggs, malted barley, liver, kidney, heart, and leafy vegetables. The richest natural source is yeast. It occurs in the free form only in the retina of the eye, in whey, and in urine; its principal forms in tissues and cells are as FMN and FAD. [NIH]

Seizures: Clinical or subclinical disturbances of cortical function due to a sudden, abnormal, excessive, and disorganized discharge of brain cells. Clinical manifestations include abnormal motor, sensory and psychic phenomena. Recurrent seizures are usually referred to as epilepsy or "seizure disorder." [NIH]

Selenium: An element with the atomic symbol Se, atomic number 34, and atomic weight 78.96. It is an essential micronutrient for mammals and other animals but is toxic in large amounts. Selenium protects intracellular structures against oxidative damage. It is an essential component of glutathione peroxidase. [NIH]

Serum: The clear portion of any body fluid; the clear fuid moistening serous membranes. 2. blood serum; the clear liquid that separates from blood on clotting. 3. immune serum; blood serum from an immunized animal used for passive immunization; an antiserum; antitoxin, or antivenin. [EU]

Spasmodic: Of the nature of a spasm. [EU]

Spastic: 1. of the nature of or characterized by spasms. 2. hypertonic, so that the muscles are stiff and the movements awkward. 3. a person exhibiting spasticity, such as occurs in spastic paralysis or in cerebral palsy. [EU]

Spectrum: A charted band of wavelengths of electromagnetic vibrations obtained by refraction and diffraction. By extension, a measurable range of activity, such as the range of bacteria affected by an antibiotic (antibacterial s.) or the complete range of manifestations of a disease. [EU]

Sporadic: Neither endemic nor epidemic; occurring occasionally in a random or isolated manner. [EU]

Stomach: An organ of digestion situated in the left upper quadrant of the abdomen between the termination of the esophagus and the beginning of the duodenum. [NIH]

Substrate: A substance upon which an enzyme acts. [EU]

Symptomatic: 1. pertaining to or of the nature of a symptom. 2. indicative (of a particular disease or disorder). 3. exhibiting the symptoms of a particular disease but having a different cause. 4. directed at the allying of symptoms, as symptomatic treatment. [EU]

Symptomatology: 1. that branch of medicine with treats of symptoms; the systematic discussion of symptoms. 2. the combined symptoms of a disease. [EU]

Synaptophysin: A 38-kDa integral membrane glycoprotein of the presynaptic vesicles in neuron and neuroendocrine cells. It is expressed by a variety of normal and neoplastic neuroendocrine cells and is therefore used as an immunocytochemical marker for neuroendocrine differentiation in various tumors. In alzheimer disease and other dementing disorders there is an important synapse loss due in part to a decrease of synaptophysin in the presynaptic vesicles. [NIH]

Thyroxine: An amino acid of the thyroid gland which exerts a stimulating effect on thyroid metabolism. [NIH]

Tinnitus: A noise in the ears, as ringing, buzzing, roaring, clicking, etc. Such sounds may at times be heard by others than the patient. [EU]

Tone: 1. the normal degree of vigour and tension; in muscle, the resistance to passive elongation or stretch; tonus. 2. a particular quality of sound or of voice. 3. to make permanent, or to change, the colour of silver stain by chemical treatment, usually with a heavy metal. [EU]

Torticollis: Wryneck; a contracted state of the cervical muscles, producing twisting of the neck and an unnatural position of the head. [EU]

Tracheostomy: Surgical formation of an opening into the trachea through the neck, or the opening so created. [NIH]

Translations: Products resulting from the conversion of one language to another. [NIH]

Vertigo: An illusion of movement; a sensation as if the external world were revolving around the patient (objective vertigo) or as if he himself were revolving in space (subjective vertigo). The term is sometimes erroneously used to mean any form of dizziness. [EU]

Viral: Pertaining to, caused by, or of the nature of virus. [EU]

Viruses: Minute infectious agents whose genomes are composed of DNA or RNA, but not both. They are characterized by a lack of independent metabolism and the inability to replicate outside living host cells. [NIH]

General Dictionaries and Glossaries

While the above glossary is essentially complete, the dictionaries listed here cover virtually all aspects of medicine, from basic words and phrases to more advanced terms (sorted alphabetically by title; hyperlinks provide rankings, information and reviews at Amazon.com):

- **Dictionary of Medical Acronymns & Abbreviations** by Stanley Jablonski (Editor), Paperback, 4th edition (2001), Lippincott Williams & Wilkins Publishers, ISBN: 1560534605, http://www.amazon.com/exec/obidos/ASIN/1560534605/icongroupinterna

- **Dictionary of Medical Terms : For the Nonmedical Person (Dictionary of Medical Terms for the Nonmedical Person, Ed 4)** by Mikel A. Rothenberg, M.D, et al, Paperback - 544 pages, 4th edition (2000), Barrons Educational Series, ISBN: 0764112015, http://www.amazon.com/exec/obidos/ASIN/0764112015/icongroupinterna

- **A Dictionary of the History of Medicine** by A. Sebastian, CD-Rom edition (2001), CRC Press-Parthenon Publishers, ISBN: 185070368X, http://www.amazon.com/exec/obidos/ASIN/185070368X/icongroupinterna

- **Dorland's Illustrated Medical Dictionary (Standard Version)** by Dorland, et al, Hardcover - 2088 pages, 29th edition (2000), W B Saunders Co, ISBN: 0721662544,
  http://www.amazon.com/exec/obidos/ASIN/0721662544/icongroupinterna

- **Dorland's Electronic Medical Dictionary** by Dorland, et al, Software, 29th Book & CD-Rom edition (2000), Harcourt Health Sciences, ISBN: 0721694934,
  http://www.amazon.com/exec/obidos/ASIN/0721694934/icongroupinterna

- **Dorland's Pocket Medical Dictionary (Dorland's Pocket Medical Dictionary, 26th Ed)** Hardcover - 912 pages, 26th edition (2001), W B Saunders Co, ISBN: 0721682812,
  http://www.amazon.com/exec/obidos/ASIN/0721682812/icongroupinterna/103-4193558-7304618

- **Melloni's Illustrated Medical Dictionary (Melloni's Illustrated Medical Dictionary, 4th Ed)** by Melloni, Hardcover, 4th edition (2001), CRC Press-Parthenon Publishers, ISBN: 85070094X,
  http://www.amazon.com/exec/obidos/ASIN/85070094X/icongroupinterna

- **Stedman's Electronic Medical Dictionary Version 5.0 (CD-ROM for Windows and Macintosh, Individual)** by Stedmans, CD-ROM edition (2000), Lippincott Williams & Wilkins Publishers, ISBN: 0781726328,
  http://www.amazon.com/exec/obidos/ASIN/0781726328/icongroupinterna

- **Stedman's Medical Dictionary** by Thomas Lathrop Stedman, Hardcover - 2098 pages, 27th edition (2000), Lippincott, Williams & Wilkins, ISBN: 068340007X,
  http://www.amazon.com/exec/obidos/ASIN/068340007X/icongroupinterna

- **Tabers Cyclopedic Medical Dictionary (Thumb Index)** by Donald Venes (Editor), et al, Hardcover - 2439 pages, 19th edition (2001), F A Davis Co, ISBN: 0803606540,
  http://www.amazon.com/exec/obidos/ASIN/0803606540/icongroupinterna

INDEX